Monet and the Impressionists for Kids

Monet

and the

Their Lives and Ideas ✦ 21 Activities

Impressionists *for* Kids

Carol Sabbeth

CHICAGO
REVIEW
PRESS

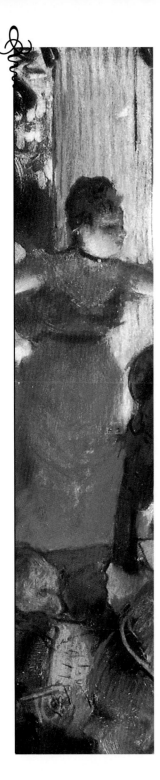

To Eileen Landstrom, a masterpiece Mom

Library of Congress Cataloging-in-Publication Data
Sabbeth, Carol, 1957–
    Monet and the impressionists for kids / Carol Landstrom Sabbeth.
        p. cm.
    Includes bibliographical references and index.
    Summary: Discusses the nineteenth-century French art movement known as Impressionism, focusing on the works of Monet, Renoir, Degas, Cassatt, Cézanne, Gauguin, and Seurat. Includes related projects and activities.
    ISBN 1-55652-397-1
    1. Impressionism (Art)—Juvenile literature. 2. Art, French—19th century—Juvenile literature. 3. Impressionist artists—France—Biography—Juvenile literature. [1. Impressionism (Art) 2. Art, French—19th century.] I. Title.

N6847.5.I4 S23 2002
759.05'4—dc21

                                                    2001047191

Cover and interior design: Joan Sommers Design

Printed in Singapore

© 2002 by Carol Sabbeth
All rights reserved
First edition
Published by Chicago Review Press, Incorporated
814 North Franklin Street
Chicago, Illinois 60610

ISBN 1-55652-397-1
5 4 3 2 1

About the Author
Carol Sabbeth presents art workshops to children and teachers throughout the United States. She recently began performing as a storyteller, impersonating the Impressionist artist Mary Cassatt. In her monologue, she tells the tale of Monet and the Impressionists. Carol is the author of *Crayons and Computers* and *Kids' Computer Creations*. She lives in Denver, Colorado, with her husband, Alex.

FRONT COVER: Left: Claude Monet, *Water Lilies*; Claude Monet, photograph H. Roger-Viollet, Paris; Right, top to bottom: Gustave Caillebotte, *Paris: A Rainy Day*; Edgar Degas, *Dancers at the Bar*; Pierre Auguste Renoir, *Two Sisters (On the Terrace)*, 1881, Oil on Canvas, 100.5 cm x 81 cm, Mr. and Mrs. Lewis Larned Coburn Memorial Collection, 1933.455, photograph courtesy of The Art Institute of Chicago.
BACK COVER: Top to bottom: Pierre Auguste Renoir, *The Ball at the Moulin de la Galette*; Mary Cassatt, *The Bath*; and Paul Cézanne, *Still Life with Curtain and Flowered Pitcher*.

Contents

About the Author iv

Acknowledgments vii

Time Line viii

Introduction xi

PART I: THE IMPRESSIONISTS

A New Way of Looking at the World 3

Art-to-Go Knapsack 19

Take a Visual Voyage 20

Impression, Me 21

Claude Monet 23

Painting the Shimmering Sky 26

Painting Reflections 30

Monet's Garden 35

Mini Haystack and Field 40

Paper Water Lily 43

Pierre Auguste Renoir 45

How to Draw a Face 50

Galette des Rois (Twelfth Night Cake) 57

Edgar Degas 59

Camera Capers 68

Mary Cassatt 71

Every Picture Tells a Story 76

Lasting Impressions 125

Picture Me   130

Picture Plugged In   130

Bingo Monet   130

Art Critic   130

PART II: THE POST-IMPRESSIONISTS

Paul Cézanne 85

Still Life à la Cézanne   90

Stenciling Cézanne   97

Paul Gauguin 99

Cup of Gauguin   107

Armchair Explorer   109

Georges Seurat 113

Seurat Sugar Cookies   123

Glossary   131

Bibliography   134

Image Credits   136

Index   139

Acknowledgments

I give many thanks to Linda Brady Tesner for her valued impression of my manuscript, and to Clarinda Hanson White, art education specialist, for sharing her ideas and experiences. Special thanks go to Cynthia Sherry and my editor, Lisa Rosenthal of Chicago Review Press. I'm also indebted to Yves Berthelot for his help with everything French; Shirley Sabbeth, museum buddy extraordinaire; and, as always, my husband, Alex, for his editing skills and enthusiasm.

Time Line

1856 Monet (at age 15) paints with Eugène Boudin

1860 Abraham Lincoln elected president of the United States

1862 Monet and Renoir meet at art school (Gleyre's studio)

1863 Salon des Refusés

Manet's *Déjeuner sur l'Herbe* causes a scandal

1866 Mary Cassatt moves to Paris (at age 22)

1867 Japanese art exhibited for the first time in the West; influences the work of Monet, Cassatt, Degas, and many other artists who will be called Impressionists

1870 Franco–Prussian War; France defeated at Sedan and Napoléon III captured

1873 Marshal MacMahon elected president of France

1874 **First Impressionist Exhibition**
Among the artists: Monet, Renoir, Degas, Cézanne, and Morisot

1876 Renoir paints *The Ball at the Moulin de la Galette*

Second Impressionist Exhibition

Alexander Graham Bell invents the telephone

1877 **Third Impressionist Exhibition**

1879 **Fourth Impressionist Exhibition**

Cézanne no longer exhibits in the Impressionist exhibitions

Cassatt joins the Impressionists

Gauguin exhibits a sculpture

Thomas A. Edison perfects the electric lightbulb

1880 **Fifth Impressionist Exhibition**

Monet and Renoir do not exhibit; instead they show work at the Salon

Gauguin exhibits paintings

1881 Sixth Impressionist Exhibition	**1887** Gottlieb Daimler builds the first automobile	**1914** World War I begins—Germany invades France
Monet and Renoir do not exhibit	**1888** George Eastman invents first hand-held snapshot camera	**1917** Edgar Degas dies (age 83)
1882 Seventh Impressionist Exhibition	**1889** Eiffel Tower built in Paris	**1918** Monet proposes to create water lily murals as gift to France in honor of WWI victory
Cassatt and Degas do not exhibit	**1891** Gauguin moves to Tahiti	
Panama Canal construction begins (completed in 1914)	Georges Seurat dies (age 31)	**1919** Pierre August Renoir dies (age 78)
1883 Monet moves to Giverny	**1903** Paul Gauguin dies (age 54)	**1926** Claude Monet dies (age 86)
Gauguin becomes a full-time artist	Wright brothers make their first successful airplane flight	Mary Cassatt dies (age 82)
1885 The Statue of Liberty sails from France to America	**1904** Mary Cassatt receives the French Legion of Honor medal	**1990** *The Ball at the Moulin de la Galette* by Renoir sells for $78.1 million
1886 Eighth (and last) Impressionist Exhibition	**1906** Paul Cézanne dies (age 67)	
Seurat exhibits pointillist style		
Monet and Renoir do not exhibit		

CLAUDE MONET

The White Water Lilies

1899

Introduction

The beautiful garden where Monet painted toward the end of his life still blooms today, over a hundred years later. If he could take you on a tour of his lush paradise, he would show you his water lily pond and the wonderful Japanese bridge he built across it. He'd point out the sparkling ripples on the sunlit water and make sure that you noticed the reflections of clouds and trees. If you were very lucky, he would set up an easel next to his own. Quietly, he would go about painting. As you watched, he'd quickly cover his canvas in loose splashes of luminous color—capturing an impression before the light changed. But you must try too! Monet's words of advice would be simple. "When you paint, try to forget what objects you have before you," he would say.

"Instead think, 'Here is a little square of blue, here an oblong of pink, here a streak of yellow,' and paint it just as it looks."

When Monet was 15 years old, an artist named Eugène Boudin painted next to him in much the same way. It was a day that would change Monet's life forever. He fell in love with nature and decided to spend the rest of his life painting it. But this way of painting—outdoors in quick impressions—was very different from what the art professors of the time were teaching. They felt that paintings should be done in a studio, carefully, with subdued colors, and—most important of all—with smooth brush strokes. When Monet went to Paris to study art, this was the obstacle he faced. Luckily, he wasn't alone in his way of thinking. There he met other

young artists who agreed with him about the future of painting.

This book follows the path of seven of these rebel artists and tells the story of their lives. It shows their struggle with the established art scene until they finally decided to hold exhibits of their own. Eventually they would hold eight independent exhibitions. There were many young artists who agreed with these rebels, but the seven who are featured in this book have one thing in common: they all took part in at least one of the eight Impressionist Exhibitions. These artists are Claude Monet (moh-NAY), Pierre Auguste Renoir (ren-WAH), Edgar Degas (day-GAH), Mary Cassatt (ka-SAHT), Paul Cézanne (say-ZAHN), Paul Gauguin (gau-GAN), and Georges Seurat (suh-RAH). Each artist had his or her individual style and idea about what subject to paint. Cézanne, Gauguin, and Seurat took Impressionism in new directions and are called Post-Impressionists. Along the way, you'll also meet other important artists like Édouard Manet and Vincent van Gogh. They were strong supporters of the movement and this new way of portraying the world in their own art, but they didn't participate in any of the Impressionist Exhibitions.

How did the Impressionists get their name? And why was their fight for recognition so difficult?

In this book you'll learn about these things and more while making fun projects along the way. Learn how to paint a landscape in Monet's style and take camera shots at unique angles just like Degas. Follow the steps to draw a portrait, like Renoir. Paint a still life using brilliant colors, just like Cézanne. There are also many games to play— using the Impressionists' art, or your own creations. Perhaps you'll find art terms that are new to you. If so, look in the glossary at the back of the book. There's also a list of Web sites that feature the Impressionist artists.

Monet and his friends lived in the late 1800s, during a time when Paris was the showcase of the world. During their lives, Paris was rebuilt as a dazzling city full of beautiful buildings, grand boulevards, and exciting cafés. Women dressed in opulent bustled gowns to attend the opera, escorted by men in white gloves and top hats. Young couples flirted at outdoor dances, or strolled down avenues lit by glowing gas lamps. These lamps inspired people to call Paris "the City of Light." Outside the city, families spent restful afternoons at the beach or picnicked in the beautiful French countryside. During the late 1800s and into the new century, Monet and his friends were there with their canvases and paints—to record the times with captured impressions.

PART I: THE IMPRESSIONISTS

PIERRE AUGUSTE RENOIR

The Ball at the Moulin de la Galette

1876

A New Way of Looking at the World

It was a warm May evening in New York City. The year was 1990. Inside, the crowd waited in anticipation. Some were there to watch, but others, noticeably more nervous, were waiting to join the action. Armed security guards stood nearby.

A hush fell in the room as the guest of honor was revealed. Its name, *Au Moulin de la Galette*, was known to everyone in the world of art. Painted 114 years earlier by Pierre Auguste Renoir, Moulin was about to go home with the highest bidder at Sotheby's auction house.

"Good evening," said John Marion, the impeccably dressed auctioneer and chairman of Sotheby's. "I'll start this at $25 million." The bidding began, and increased in increments of $1 million. With each bid the excitement grew as the crowd of art world movers and shakers sensed that history was about to be made. As the price rose above $40 million, they gasped, and a duel began between two telephone bidders. With phones to their ears, Sotheby's personnel relayed their clients' wishes, each one raising the stakes higher and higher. In the end, one of the most famous paintings in the world was sold for $78.1 million. It was the second-highest price ever paid for a painting. The sale took only 5 ½ minutes.

If only its creator could have known! A little more than a hundred years earlier, and an ocean away, the doors opened to an art exhibit that received a very different kind of welcome.

The Exhibition Opens

On April 15, 1874, an art exhibit opened that featured some of the most beautiful, well-loved paintings in the world—well loved today, that is. In 1874, the artists couldn't even give their paintings away. The problem at the 1874 exhibit was simple: these paintings were different from what people were used to. Critics warned pregnant women that their unborn babies would become ill just by entering the doors of the exhibit. The artists took turns standing guard because they worried the paintings would be slashed by an outraged art teacher or showered with tomatoes by a collector gone mad.

"Madness" was mentioned more than once when the critics wrote about the event. One journalist claimed that a visitor began biting everyone in sight after seeing the exhibition. Another visitor thought he knew the secret of the artists' technique: they loaded a gun with paint and fired it at the canvas, and to finish it off, they added their signature. This joke was repeated all over Paris.

A painting of a harbor scene at sunrise especially outraged one critic, Louis Leroy. Its title was *Impression, Sunrise*. Jokingly, he called this group of rebel artists Impressionists. It wasn't meant to be a compliment.

Upsetting the Citizens

There is another reason why the art of the Impressionists received such a hostile welcome in France. The First Impressionist Exhibition opened during a time when France was recovering from many tragic events. The country had just been at war with Prussia, its neighbor to the east, which is now part of Germany. Casualties from the war, and the unstable government after France was defeated, resulted in the deaths of thousands of French men, women, and children. After the turmoil ended, the people of France wanted to feel safe and secure again. To many, that meant going back to the way things used to be before all the trouble. The Impressionists style did not help them feel better. Citizens weren't ready for more unsettling ideas and events, even though these ideas applied only to art. Art was seen as an indicator of the

> The highest price ever paid for a painting was $82.5 million. Painted by Vincent van Gogh, its title is *Portrait of Dr. Gachet*. It was bought by a Japanese businessman named Ryoei Saito. Two days later, he bought *Au Moulin de la Galette*.
>
> "It wasn't a big shopping trip. . . . For paintings like that, the price was cheap."
>
> —Japanese businessman Ryoei Saito regarding his $160.6 million purchases

CLAUDE MONET

Impression, Sunrise

1872–73

moral health of the nation and was therefore expected to play its part in the reconstruction of the French nation.

Art of the Past

Long ago, the only people wealthy enough to buy art were church officials and kings and queens. If artists wanted to make a living, they had to paint subjects that would appeal to their buyers' tastes. The churches wanted paintings that showed scenes from the Bible. Paintings with titles such as *Madonna and Child with Angels* were popular. Kings and queens liked battle scenes—these reminded them of how powerful they were. For decoration they enjoyed scenes from mythology— chubby cupids and lounging goddesses. Most of these paintings from earlier times were very large—large enough to fill the walls of palaces, churches, and state buildings.

Eventually, more people became wealthy enough to buy artwork, but their tastes were similar to those of the royalty. (They wanted to feel like kings and queens, too!) The 1850s and 1860s were an economic boom time in Paris. From bankers to builders, and all those who supplied them, more people in France had money to spend. They commissioned artists to paint family portraits, and they also considered large scenes of historical events to be in good taste. They continued to enjoy

their paintings of goddesses as well. Most often the goddesses portrayed in art did not wear clothes. Society at the time accepted paintings of nude women, but only if the women were placed in appropriate settings. A picture of a beautiful woman dramatically posed unclothed atop an ocean wave might be titled *Birth of Venus*. This was art. On the other hand, a picture of a similar woman lounging on a modern French couch would be considered scandalous. This, most people thought, was pornography.

The Salon

From the 1600s to the 1800s there was only one place for wealthy art lovers to buy art: at an exhibition called the Salon. In Monet's time, the Salon was held in a huge glass-roofed exhibition hall called the Palais de l'Industrie. Each year, as many as 4,000 works of art were chosen by a jury to be shown at the Salon. The jury was made up of professors from the most famous art school in the Western world, the École des Beaux-Arts ("School of Fine Arts"). These professors felt it was important to uphold traditions, not create new ones. They preferred works that were painted in a style that had been used for hundreds of years. The best paintings, in their opinion, were done on large canvases, using subdued colors and well-blended brush strokes.

The Salon lasted two months each year and was visited by art dealers, collectors, and critics from all over the world. A panel of judges awarded prizes to paintings they thought were outstanding. The winning artists would often be commissioned by wealthy patrons to paint special pieces such as portraits. To be a successful artist meant to be successful at the Salon.

Because of the Salon's importance, every artist hoped to be included in the exhibit. Each year all the artists gathered their best pieces and brought them to be judged. If they were lucky, their pieces would be chosen. Artwork that the jury especially liked was hung *on the line*, or at eye level. Art considered inferior was *skyed*, or hung high above eye level where it could hardly be seen. Still, being skyed was better than the alternative—to be rejected. Rejected Salon paintings were returned with a large *R* stamped on the back of the canvas. An artist had to hide the *R* with a new backing in order to sell the painting later. No one wanted to buy a painting that had been refused by the Salon!

The Salon des Refusés

In 1863, when Monet and most of his friends were still studying at art school, a very special Salon was held. That year, the jury was especially severe, accepting only 2,217 works out of the 5,000 that were submitted. The artists whose works were not accepted protested so strongly that Emperor Napoléon III gave in to their wishes. He decided to let the public be the jury that year, and he ordered all the rejected paintings to be exhibited as well. The paintings were hung in a separate part of the exhibition hall, in rooms that came to be called the *Salons des Refusés* ("Salon of the Rejected"). More crowds than usual came to the Salon that year. One painting in particular, *Le Déjeuner sur l'Herbe* (Luncheon on the Grass), drew their attention. It was a picnic scene painted by Édouard Manet. In it, Manet had painted a woman picnicker who is sitting on the grass. The unusual thing is that she is naked. She's staring directly out at the viewer, completely ignoring the two clothed gentlemen sitting with her. The painting created a huge scandal. "What kind of picnic is this?" the public

"A monkey who has got hold of a box of paints."
—Review of Impressionist art by French newspaper, 1875

"I am very happy. Once you like something, go all the way."
—Japanese businessman Ryoei Saito regarding his $160.6 million purchase of Renoir and Van Gogh paintings, 1990

demanded. As for Monet and his artist friends, the art of Manet inspired them. Not only was the subject modern, but the way Manet had applied the paint in loose, unblended brush strokes thrilled Monet and the other art students.

Rejected Too Often

The artists now known as the Impressionists became very good at putting new backings on their rejected paintings. At times, one of their paintings would be accepted—if done in the traditional style. The Salon judges wanted noble scenes, dark and well blended. The Impressionists' everyday scenes, painted outdoors, upset them. They were unable to think of the small canvases, filled with quick, loose, brightly colored brush strokes, as art. Eventually, Monet and his friends gave up trying to convince the Salon judges and decided to hold their own exhibition.

Planning the First Exhibition

The Impressionist artists did not always agree with one another, but most of them had one thing in common: they preferred to paint during the day. This way they could capture the sunlight as it lit up their subjects. Once the sun set and they could no longer paint, Monet and his friends would meet at one of the local cafés to talk about their work. Sitting under the gaslights, they excitedly discussed and debated their ideas about art and planned their escape from the Salon. They were tired of having their art rejected for the exhibition, so they decided to hold their own. One member of the group, a photographer named Félix Tournachon (known as Nadar), offered his studio on Boulevard des Capucines for the show. They decided it would open on April 15, but they couldn't agree on a name for their group. The artists had individual styles and didn't want too limiting a name. Some thought "Independents" would be a good name, while others preferred "Intransigents." Even the French name for a nasturtium flower, "La Capucine," was suggested. (It was also the name of the street where the exhibit would be held.) The artist who suggested it, Edgar Degas, thought the pretty yellow-orange flower would make a good logo on the posters announcing the exhibition. Finally they decided to call themselves "A Limited Company of Painters, Sculptors, and Engravers."

The Rebel Artists

The 30 artists who made up the Company were as different in personality as they were in their art.

Their leader, Claude Monet, was very outspoken—as bold as his colorful canvases. Once the exhibition was planned, he decided to paint a picture especially for the show. Its purpose was to demonstrate his ideas about painting. Before the exhibition opened, Monet stood at a window in Nadar's studio and painted a picture of the busy Paris street down below. Because the people walking on the street were far away, he painted them without details in small, dark splashes. When visitors came to the exhibit, Monet thought, they could compare his painting with what they saw out the window. Then they would understand!

Unfortunately, they didn't understand at all. When the show opened, the critics just made fun of Monet's painting. "Here is an impression which baffles me," one wrote. "Please tell me the meaning of these innumerable black dribbles at the bottom of the canvas." (He was referring to the pedestrians.) Monet got even more attention with another picture in the exhibition. It was his painting (*Impression, Sunrise*) that inspired the same critic to rename Monet's group. He called them Impressionists. Whether they liked it or not, the Limited Company of Painters, Sculptors, and Engravers had a new name.

Some artists in the group would not become famous, but many of them would. There was Pierre Auguste Renoir, whose personality was as sunny as his paintings. Renoir was a people person—and he made all his subjects look simply marvelous. This is obvious in one of the paintings he chose for the exhibition. Titled *La Loge*, it's a portrait of a beau-

CLAUDE MONET
Boulevard des Capucines
1873–74

EDGAR DEGAS

Dancers Preparing for an Audition
c. 1880

tiful woman who is attending the opera. She's dazzling in her lace gown and jewels. "Why shouldn't art be pretty?" Renoir said. "There are enough unpleasant things in the world."

Almost his opposite was Edgar Degas, an often gruff and arrogant man. He chose to paint indoor subjects. Degas didn't try to hide his feelings about painting outdoors. "Don't tell me about those fellows cluttering the fields with their easels. . . . The stupid fools, crouching out there over their stupid shields of white canvas," he warned. Degas created many paintings of young ballerinas hard at work and of local singers entertaining at café-concerts. Degas chose one painting for the exhibition called *Rehearsal of a Ballet on Stage.* In it young ballerinas wear white gauzy tutus and practice their dance steps. One dancer standing at the edge of the painting is partially cropped off—only part of her body is shown. This is how a photograph might have captured the scene. The camera had just been invented, and Degas liked the way photographs cut off images in unusual ways. Many of his colorful paintings show the influence of photography.

There was also a Frenchwoman in the group, Berthe Morisot. Morisot came from an upper-class family. She had to be content with painting scenes of life in the home because, in 1874, "respectable" young ladies were not allowed to go out about town unchaperoned. What's more, they were not supposed to become professional artists. One of the paintings she chose to exhibit is titled *The Cradle*. It's a picture of her sister Edma looking lovingly at her newborn baby. Morisot and later an American woman named Mary Cassatt would be among the best Impressionist artists.

And then there was Paul Cézanne, who, according to Cassatt, "looked like a cut-throat with large red eyeballs standing out from his head in a most ferocious manner." Not caring much for people, Cézanne preferred to paint things that stood still—mountains and bowls of fruit pleased him. One of the paintings he chose for the exhibition is of a house set in a hilly village. The painting's title is *House of the Hanged Man*. As time went on, Cézanne disagreed with many of the Impressionists' ideas and developed a technique very much his own.

BERTHE MORISOT

The Cradle

1872

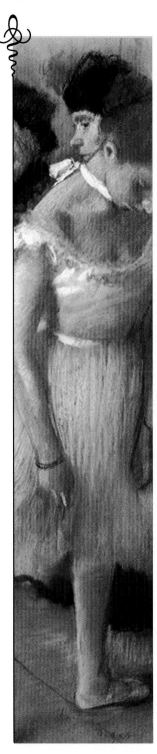

Life in Paris— Impressionist Scenes

Monet and his friends lived during an exciting time in Paris. The city had recently been renovated and was now a thriving, modern place to live and work. And it was a place to play! Monet and his artist friends captured the energy by painting their impressions of this dazzling city.

The renovation began in the 1850s, when Monet was still a young boy. At the time, Paris was a medieval city. The sewer system was poor, and drinking water was scarce. At night, the narrow, winding streets were dark and scary. In 1852, Napoléon III became emperor and set out to change all that. He decided to make Paris the showpiece of Europe. With the help of his chief city official, Baron Haussmann, Napoléon III leveled the old city and built a modern metropolis. Haussmann designed long, wide boulevards and lined them with beautiful buildings. He lighted the avenues with 32,000 gas lamps. People fondly called Paris the "City of Light."

New cafés and restaurants sprang up along the avenues. Because the sidewalks were so wide, chairs and tables could be set up outdoors. This invited Parisians (and artists) to sit for hours, watching as richly dressed men and women strolled past. Taking a leisurely walk along the boulevard was a popular pastime. There was even a name for this type of activity. A wealthy, well-dressed man who strolled the streets, observing life with cool detachment, was called a *flaneur*. The trademark of the flaneur was his black top hat. It was said that a flaneur's favorite pet was the turtle, because it kept the same pace as its owner.

For those more energetic, there was dancing. "Dancing (in Paris) is a function of life," wrote an American observer. Public dances, often held on outdoor patios, were among the most popular forms of Parisian entertainment. A lively provocative dance called the cancan was all the rage. Women danced with wild abandon, high-kicking to fast music and holding up their skirts to show their legs—unheard-of at the time. Men joined in, too. At the end, they dropped to the floor, doing a split. Other couples preferred to whirl around to the popular waltzes.

Parisians also enjoyed professional dance performances. Baron Haussmann's new opera house was very popular for its Opera-Ballets. The theater was a place to see and be seen. Diamond-clad women in opulent, bustled dresses sat high in balconies, while the men sat below and kept busy looking up with small binoculars called opera glasses. At times, it seemed as if no one was paying attention to what was happening on the stage!

GUSTAVE CAILLEBOTTE

Paris: A Rainy Day

1877

Backstage, Edgar Degas often sketched the ballerinas as they stretched and rehearsed.

On Sunday afternoons, some young people went to places like the Moulin de la Galette just to chat and flirt. Pierre Auguste Renoir loved to go there too, and merrymakers enjoyed seeing him. He became a familiar sight, looking at them from behind his large canvas. Artists seemed to be everywhere capturing the energy and painting their impressions of this dazzling city.

Café-concerts were another popular place for entertainment. Here, people from all social classes mixed. This was unusual because wealthy Parisians seldom socialized with working-class people. The Folies-Bergère was one of the Impressionists' favorite places to paint the café-concert crowd. There was so much going on! Throughout the night, entertainers sang rowdy songs, professional dancers kicked up lively renditions of the cancan, and trapeze artists swung from the ceiling. Édouard Manet painted Suzon, a barmaid who worked at the Folies, and made her famous forever. Other people are also at work in this painting, *Bar at the Folies-Bergère*. If you look in the top left corner, you'll see the pink-stockinged legs and bright green shoes of a trapeze artist.

IMPRESSIONIST MUSIC

The Impressionist painters weren't alone in thinking about art in a new way. Some musicians tried to imitate light and color using new techniques, too. Orchestral music could create the illusion of color by using the different instruments in unusual combinations. French composers like Maurice Ravel and Claude Debussy wrote piano music that lets us hear light flashing and glimmering. Today they are known as Impressionist composers.

A lovely folk legend tells the story of Ondine, a water nymph. She falls in love with a brave knight. Her fellow spirits warn her that love between a spirit and a human is bound to create problems, but she marries him anyway. Ravel wrote piano music inspired by this story. He makes us hear the murmuring of the streams and the sparkling of the light on the water's surface. Listen to Ravel's *Ondine* and see if you agree.

The Dark Side of the City of Light

Life in Paris was not glamorous for everyone. When Baron Haussmann rebuilt Paris, it was at the cost of many of the city's poor. Twenty thousand houses were demolished and 350,000 people displaced. The working classes were forced to migrate to the outskirts of the city, to poor, run-down suburbs. Meanwhile, the affluent middle classes moved into Haussmann's elegant new buildings.

But even in the city itself, there was a dark side. Most people would have preferred not to notice them. But the sad, unhealthy aspects of Paris didn't escape some of the Impressionists' canvases. There are many paintings that show the loneliness and desolation that can be found in a big city. One increasing problem was alcoholism. A popular drink called absinthe only made the problem worse. Favored by working-class men and women, it was so strong it was eventually banned. Degas captured the effects of this powerful liquor in his painting *Absinthe*. In this painting two shabbily dressed café regulars stare vacantly over their drinks. Degas also painted images of laundresses as they sweated over their ironing boards, preparing the gowns that would be worn by the rich—perhaps to Haussmann's new opera house.

EDGAR DEGAS
Detail from *Cafe-Concert at the Ambassadeurs*
c. 1875–77

Capturing Modern Images

The artists who came to be known as the Impressionists shared one common goal: to depict modern life—the world around them as they saw it. They wanted to present a realistic view with nothing edited out. They called it a "slice of life." Each artist had his or her own idea about what type of slice of life to present.

ÉDOUARD MANET
Bar at the Folies-Bergère
1881–82

THE BARBIZON SCHOOL

The Impressionists weren't the first group of artists to leave their studio to study nature directly. They were following in the footsteps of a group of artists who had painted since the 1840s. These painters, such as Camille Corot, made their works in the forests around Barbizon, a village about 30 miles southeast of Paris, and were known as the Barbizon School. Their paintings expressed the solitude and quiet of nature. Barbizon artists painted in misty shades of gray, green, and earth tones. Their style was very different from the brightly colored, light-filled scenes painted by the Impressionists.

Many artists, such as Monet and Renoir, took their canvases outdoors, *en plein air* ("in the open air"). They wanted to paint nature directly. These artists were fascinated by the sunlight and shadow as it danced across their subject. They recorded their "impressions" with quick dabs of their brush, making colorful commas and vibrant dashes.

City dwellers enjoyed spending time outdoors, too. Many people could afford weekend excursions because jobs were plentiful and wages were high. Because of a newly built railway system, Parisians were able to enjoy a picnic at the beach or a boat ride at a riverside resort. The Impressionists were there, too, to capture the moment. One picture that Monet painted of his family at the beach actually has sand sticking to it.

Newly available materials allowed artists to set up shop wherever they wished. One new tool was called a French easel. It was a small, handy box that unfolded into a stand. The box contained a palette, holder, paints, and brushes—a complete painting kit. Metal tubes began to be used to hold paint. Previously, oil paints were stored in little pouches made from pigs' bladders. The painter pierced the skin with a tack, squeezed out the paint, and used the tack as a plug. Unfortunately, the paint hardened after a while. The new metal tubes were much more dependable. The paints were improved too, coming in brighter, more vivid colors. This new portable equipment made painting outdoors much easier for the Impressionists. And each, in his or her own way, showed the world what could be done with it.

A Time for Change

Paris was alive with new ideas in the late 1800s. Although still recovering from a devastating war and an unstable government, Parisians could enjoy more freedoms than ever before. It was a time for change, and the young Impressionists were full of new ideas. From 1874 to 1886 they held eight Impressionist Exhibitions. Over these 12 years,

THE OTHER ART OF THE DAY

The Impressionists weren't the only artists to think big. In 1885, eleven years after the First Impressionist Exhibition, a ship set sail from the coast of France. The most important passenger aboard was an elegant lady on her way to America. Her lovely nose was $4\frac{1}{2}$ feet long and her waist was a slender 35 feet. When assembled, she reached 151 feet, 1 inch, from the tip of her toes to the torch she held in her raised right hand. Her name was Liberty.

Designed by a young French sculptor named Frédéric Auguste Bartholdi, the Statue of Liberty was a gift to America from the people of France. The man who first thought of this gift was Édouard de Laboulaye. Laboulaye was a prominent French politician and historian who wanted to celebrate America's democratic government. This was something France didn't have when Laboulaye first thought of the statue in 1865. At the time, Napoléon III was emperor—someone who didn't believe in a democratic government. To avoid problems with the Emperor, Laboulaye had to wait until Napoléon III was no longer in power. With money donated from French citizens, the making of Lady Liberty began. The year was 1874, the same year as the First Impressionist Exhibition.

The artist who designed Liberty rented the largest studio he could find for the construction of the huge statue. As the work progressed, taking a stroll over to the studio became a popular pastime for many Parisians. Inquisitive visitors were sometimes baffled by what they saw. A giant hand might lie in one corner, a foot in another, and a string of toes in yet another. Slowly, piece by piece, Liberty took shape. Finally, in 1884, she stood completed in a Paris street, towering over the surrounding buildings. In order to ship her, she was disassembled and packed in 214 crates. After a train ride to the coast, she was loaded aboard a navy ship for her trip to America. Today, a smaller version of the statue stands in Paris, facing her sister to the west.

younger artists joined the group, adding their own ideas about painting. The Impressionists' art was scorned for many years, but in the end they won their battle. By the time most of the artists reached their 50s they had become wealthy from sales of their work. Today, millions of visitors flock to museums to see their art. For this, each artist had to work very hard and suffer much criticism. The following chapters tell the story of how each artist finally won recognition.

ÉDOUARD MANET

On the Beach at Boulogne
1868

Art-to-Go Knapsack

Because of the new portable art supplies, the Impressionists were able to wander the countryside looking for new scenes to capture. Strollers out on a sunny afternoon might see Monet scurrying up the path carrying his portable easel. Following close behind would be his stepdaughter Blanche pushing a wheelbarrow full of canvases. Cézanne carried his supplies in a small wooden box strapped to his back like a knapsack. Put together your own kit and take it with you when you paint en plein air.

What to include in your kit:

Clipboard with blank paper

Watercolor crayons or pencils

Watercolor paints

Paintbrush

Pencil eraser

Small plastic container for water

Crayons or markers

Art-to-Go Knapsack (see activity below)

Materials

Pillowcase
Ruler
Pencil
Straight pins
Needle
Thread
Scissors
2 pieces 30-inch (75 cm) cord

1. Turn the pillowcase inside out and using the ruler to make it straight, draw a line 18 inches (45 cm) from the open edge of the case. Pin the layers together along this marked line. Sew the layers together along the line. Remove the pins and cut across the pillowcase 1/2 inch below the stitches. Set aside the excess fabric from the bottom of the case. Turn the shortened pillowcase right side out.

2. Cut 2 small slots, one at each bottom corner of the pillowcase. Be sure to cut through both the bottom and the top layer of the case. At the top of the case, the fabric comes folded over. At each upper corner, cut a slot in the top layer of fabric only. Turn the case over and repeat. You'll have a total of 4 slots at the top.

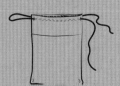

3. Starting on the right side, thread one piece of cord into the slot at the top. Pull it out the slot on the left. (Hint: To thread cord through the slots, tape one end to a pencil and pull it through.) Turn the case over and repeat. Tie the loose ends through the slot at the bottom. This will make a carrying strap. Repeat for the opposite corner of the pillowcase, starting at the opposite side. Close the knapsack by pulling on each strap.

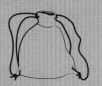

CLAUDE MONET

Detail from *Boulevard des Capucines*

1873–74

Take a Visual Voyage

When you look at a painting, you'll notice more details if you follow a visual path through the artwork. This game guides you on a tour through part of Renoir's The Ball at the Moulin de la Galette. *Look at the entire painting on page 2 and see what else you can find.*

1. Start the tour through a picture at the foreground. In this painting you'll notice two young women looking off to the right. Next, let your eyes scan the middle distance of the picture. A dancing couple has noticed you looking at them—they seem to be inviting you to come join them. End your visual tour by looking at the background of the picture. We know that this is an outdoor scene because we see trees and lampposts.

2. Did you notice these scenes along your journey?

   In the foreground: a little girl talking to a woman

   In the middle distance: a man in a hat kissing his partner on her cheek

   In the background: a couple quarreling

Another Impression: Take this visual voyage whenever you look at a painting. You'll be amazed at how many more things you notice. See if your friends can pick out the detail you like best. It's fun to notice where everyone is looking if there are people in the picture. Maybe someone is looking at you!

PIERRE AUGUSTE RENOIR

Detail from *The Ball at the Moulin de la Galette*
1876

Activity

Impression, Me

If you look carefully at Monet's painting Impression, Sunrise *on page 5, you'll see that it's made up of many short, choppy, unblended strokes of color. These dabs and dashes only blend together when seen from a distance.*

"When you paint, try to forget what objects you have before you, a tree, a house, a field, or whatever. Instead think, 'Here is a little square of blue, here an oblong of pink, here a streak of yellow,' and paint it just as it looks."—Claude Monet

Make your own Impressionist picture using Monet's ideas.

Materials

Old magazines
Scissors
Cotton swabs
Acrylic paints

1. Cut out a large photograph of a landscape or seascape from a magazine.

2. Look carefully at the picture. Notice that what at first appears as one solid color is really a combination of colors. For instance, fluffy white clouds might also have lavender, gray, and yellow in them. The blue water of a lake may be made up of many hues of blue, green, and purple. If the sun is setting, you may even find pink in the color of the water.

3. Dip a cotton swab into one color of paint. Add color to the photo by making bold, short strokes with the swab on top of the picture. Use a clean swab for each color you add. Keep each stroke crisp, being careful not to blend the colors together. Continue until the entire picture is painted in short, separate splashes of color. Think of a catchy title for your picture starting with: Impression, _____.

CLAUDE MONET

Detail from *Impression, Sunrise*
1872–73

CLAUDE MONET

Cliff-walk at Pourville

1882

Claude Monet

The same year the Statue of Liberty sailed away from the coast of France, 44-year-old Claude Monet explored its rocky shores. He planned to capture the sunlight as it lit up a hidden cove along the Normandy coast. The cove could only be reached at low tide, when the water became shallow enough to cross. He consulted a tide table to determine when the low tide would occur and checked a chart showing the sun's position at that time. It was important for the sunlight to be at just the right angle for the effect he wanted.

At exactly the right moment he scampered across the slimy rocks with his canvas, easel, brushes, and paint box strapped to his back. He quickly set up his easel and began to paint. Concentrating on the sparkling view, he didn't notice the tide coming back in. Suddenly, a giant wave crashed against the shore, showering him, his brushes, and a palette full of paint with salt water. The painting and all his materials were lost. And so, he thought, was he. But he managed to survive, his beard covered in a tapestry of blues and yellows. On this particular day, nature decided to paint Monet. It took days to get the paint out of his beard!

Growing Up in Le Havre

Oscar Claude Monet was used to crashing waves—he grew up at the ocean. Monet was born in Paris on November 14, 1840, and his family moved to Le Havre when he was five years old. Monet's aunt and uncle already lived in Le Havre, and his parents joined them in their wholesale grocery business.

Le Havre is a seaport town on the northern coast of France, and the Monets' successful grocery store supplied the ships that docked in the port. Le Havre is in a region called Normandy, which is famous for its busy harbor, smelly cheeses, and wonderful apple wine.

Monet loved the sea. He hiked along the cliffs overlooking the water and knew every jetty and beach around Le Havre. He didn't care much for indoor activities—including going to school. "I was born unruly," he admitted later. "I could never bend to any rule, even as a very small child . . . the school always seemed to me like a prison." The only lessons Monet really enjoyed were his drawing lessons. His favorite type of drawing has an unusual name: caricature. A *caricature* is a funny drawing of a person that exaggerates or distorts what the person looks like. Monet didn't do very well in school, but he had fun drawing caricatures of all his teachers.

He enjoyed wandering along the beaches, making caricatures of the tourists. People loved them! They bought his drawings for 10 to 20 francs (about $60 today). That was more than his teachers earned in a day. "If I had continued, I would be a millionaire," Monet said when he was an old man. When he was 15 years old he began to exhibit his caricatures in the window of a local art supply store. Monet would visit the shop for the joy of hearing passersby admire his work. "I almost burst out of my skin with pride," he later recalled.

The store also displayed paintings by an older artist, Eugène Boudin. They were small canvases filled with brilliantly colored landscapes. Boudin painted them *en plein air*. At the time, most painters worked indoors—art schools didn't even teach landscape painting. Art teachers admitted that quick sketches made *en plein air* could be useful, but they insisted that students should bring these sketches back to the studio and complete them there. That way, they could edit the scene and change the colors so that they were more artistically pleasing. That usually meant dark, subdued tones. Boudin felt differently. He thought artists should paint outdoors, not in a stuffy, dark studio. That way the scenes would seem more real. "They are so beautiful, the sea and the sky, the animals, just as nature made them, their real way of being, in the light, in the air, just as they are," he said.

Painting Nature

One day Boudin invited Monet to join him in painting at the beach. Monet wasn't so sure he wanted to go. He liked to draw, not paint. Besides, like many others in Le Havre, he didn't really care for Boudin's little paintings—they were so different. He did like the ocean, though, so Monet bought a box of paints and went to the seaside with Boudin. He watched Boudin set up his easel and start to paint. Monet was mesmerized by how the older man slowly captured on canvas the look and feel of the beautiful countryside. "Suddenly, it was as though a veil had been ripped from my eyes," Monet remembered. His life would never be the same. "I grasped what painting could be . . . my destiny as a painter opened up before me." As Monet worked beside Boudin, he realized how wonderful it was to paint outdoors. "I understood nature and I learned at the same time to love it." This love affair would last a lifetime.

Monet was 15 years old when he decided he'd like to be a painter. But first he had to finish school. Meanwhile, he painted with Boudin whenever he could. Sadly, his mother died during this time. Because Monet didn't get along with his father, he moved in with his aunt, Marie-Jeanne Lecadre. Among many other things, his father did not encourage Monet's enthusiasm for art. His father would have preferred that he start learning about the family business. But his aunt was an amateur painter herself and took special interest in her nephew and his drawing.

When Monet turned 18 he announced his decision to become an artist. Boldly, he asked his father to give him an allowance while he studied in Paris. The answer came quickly. "You shall have not a penny." But Monet was determined. He replied, "I will get along without it!"

CLAUDE MONET
The Stroll, Camille Monet and her Son Jean
(Woman with a Parasol)
1875

25

Painting the Shimmering Sky

Monet loved to paint clouds. If you look closely at the wispy swirls in his painting The Stroll, *you'll discover many different colors in the clouds.*

Materials

2 sheets drawing paper	Paintbrush
Pencil	Container of water
Crayons	Scissors
Watercolor paints	Glue stick

1. Draw a horizon line lightly in pencil, about a quarter of the way up from the bottom of your picture.

2. Using a white crayon, draw wispy cloud shapes above the horizon line. (You won't see the strokes on the white paper.) Add crayon splashes of other colors that you see in Monet's clouds, such as yellow and lavender.

3. Paint the sky with watercolors. Clouds will appear as the crayon resists the paint.

4. Look at Monet's grassy hilltop on the previous pages. How many colors do you see? Notice the highlights of yellow as the sun bounces off the grass. Paint the area below the horizon line with short dashes of these colors.

5. On a separate sheet of paper, draw the outline of an image. It might be a person, tree, house, or animal. Paint the image without very much detail and let it dry. Cut out the image and glue it onto your other picture.

6. Look closely at how Monet made his shadow of the woman in *The Stroll*. The shadow is dark, but not gray or black. Its shape is similar to the outline of the woman's dress because her body is blocking the sunlight and casting the shadow. Add a shadow to your picture.

CLAUDE MONET

Detail from *The Stroll, Camille Monet and her Son Jean (Woman with a Parasol)*

Off to Paris

Using the money he had saved from selling carica-tures, Monet left home to study in Paris. When he arrived he looked for an art school. The official school was the École des Beaux-Arts. The École focused on styles used by artists almost 200 years earlier. The academy approved of paintings that had dark, moody colors. Brush strokes were so smooth you couldn't even see them. The school existed to preserve traditions, not to create new ones.

Monet refused to study at the official school. He knew that his style of painting was something for the future, not the past. Instead, he took les-sons at a private studio called the Académie Suisse. It was one of the free studios in Paris where artists could chip in to pay for a model and work without advice or criticism from a teacher.

Two years later, Monet's studies came to a halt. He had reached an age when young men in France had to sign up for a military draft. The draft worked like a lottery. If Monet drew an unlucky number, he would be drafted for seven years of service. Monet was unlucky; his plans to study art would have to be put on hold.

Monet was offered another choice that would have kept him out of the military. It was possible for young men to buy their way out of military duty by paying a substitute to take their place. Monet's father offered to buy his way out—but there was one condition. Monet would have to give up painting and come back to Le Havre and work in the family business. Monet refused.

Monet joined an infantry unit that was based in Africa. But he didn't stay long. After a year he caught typhoid fever and was sent home to recover. When it came time for Monet to return to duty, his aunt agreed to buy his way out of the military—with no conditions.

Monet Returns

Monet was more determined than ever to return to Paris. This time, with help from his aunt, Monet was able to pressure his father into providing an allowance. After all, hadn't Monet already been successful in selling his caricatures? Surely after a little training he'd be able to sell many paintings at the Salon. Reluctantly, his father agreed. But he had a requirement—he expected Monet to seek entrance to the École des Beaux-Arts. "I wish to see you in a studio, working under the discipline of a well-known master," his father told him. Monet, however, had other plans.

When Monet returned to Paris he studied with a Swiss painter named Charles Gleyre. Gleyre was a master at the École des Beaux-Arts, but he also

CLAUDE MONET

Regattas at Argenteuil
1872

had a private studio that was only loosely connected with the school. Gleyre was the most lenient of the independent art teachers. Monet kept this fact hidden from his father. At the studio, Monet made friends with other artists who shared his ideas about the future of painting. Three of them, Frédéric Bazille, Pierre Auguste Renoir, and Alfred Sisley, would also become famous Impressionist artists.

Often, Monet would invite his artist friends to join him for a visit to the country. They would set up their portable easels and paint the great outdoors. This was the way to learn about painting, Monet thought. After 17 months at Gleyre's studio, where he had the opportunity to paint outdoors whenever he wished, Gleyre grew ill and was forced to close his studio. Instead of finding another teacher, Monet and his group decided to strike out on their own.

Monet's Methods

To Monet, the most important part of painting was capturing the sparkling colors of light. It was exciting to paint them because they changed so quickly. Monet was a master at it! His bold brush strokes and colors give you the feeling of being right there at the moment he created the painting.

He painted directly on the canvas. This was not the way most artists painted. Usually they made practice drawings first. Monet believed in capturing the scene immediately, before the light had a chance to change. He always wore dark clothes so he wouldn't reflect light onto the canvas, and he perched an umbrella over his canvas. It helped him apply the right colors, without the glare of the sun. Sometimes he carried several canvases with him. As the light changed during the day, he could paint a scene in different ways. He had to work fast. The angle of the sun was very important to Monet. Once his friend Ambroise Vollard came upon Monet while out walking. "I saw a little car arriving in a cloud of dust. Monet gets out of it, looks at the sun, and consults his watch. 'I'm half an hour late,' he says, 'I'll come back tomorrow.'"

It didn't have to be a nice warm day in order for Monet to paint outdoors. He looked for impressions in all sorts of weather. One time a journalist spotted him after a snowstorm, painting outdoors in the freezing cold. "We noticed a foot-warmer, then an easel, then a man, swathed in three coats, his hands in gloves, his face half-frozen. It was Monet, studying a snow effect."

Most of all Monet loved to paint pictures of rivers and ponds—especially when he could show reflections in the water. Many of these were painted from his little boat. Stocked with paints, canvases, and drawing supplies, it was a floating art studio. He could paddle it through the water, looking for the perfect viewpoint.

Meeting at the Café Guerbois

Paris was an exciting place to live! It was the art capital of the world. Artists from all over came to Paris to study. During the day they painted, and as soon as the sun went down they joined together to talk about their work. Many nights Monet went to the Café Guerbois, the local hangout of several young artists. Excitedly, they would discuss and debate. They all had their own ideas about how, what, and where to paint. Monet thought that artists should work outdoors, painting quick impressions of the landscape. The scene might be of a beautiful sunset, and if chimneys were in the background belching out pollution, they must also

Painting Reflections

Monet was interested in painting reflections in the water. His long, horizontal dashes of color in Regattas at Argenteuil *show us that there was a lazy breeze on the river.*

Materials

Light blue and dark blue
  construction paper
Scissors
Glue stick

Colored chalk
Spray water bottle
Coin

1. Fold the dark blue piece of construction paper in half and cut along the fold. Glue one of the cut pieces to the bottom half of the light blue piece of construction paper. Put the other half of dark paper aside; it will not be used.

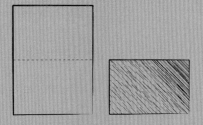

2. Place the page so that the light blue paper is at the top. Color an outdoor scene on the light blue paper using chalk.

3. Lightly mist the entire piece of art with water. Fold the page in half, so that the image on the light blue half covers the dark blue paper. Rub the folded paper with the edge of a coin. Unfold the artwork and let it dry.

4. The reflected image in your artwork is now an impression captured on a calm day, when the water is smooth. To show ripples, make horizontal dashes in the reflection, using blue chalk.

CLAUDE MONET

Detail from *Regattas at Argenteuil*

be captured as well. His good friend Renoir disagreed. The ugly chimneys must not be shown! Only beautiful things should be painted. Degas, a rather unpleasant man, liked the idea of showing unpleasant things. But only a fool would paint outdoors! And so it went . . . every one was sure that he was correct. Art critics and writers also joined in. They had their opinions, too. Despite strong disagreements, Monet loved these meetings. "Nothing could have been more stimulating than these debates with the constant clashes of opinions," he said.

There was one thing on which they all could agree: if their work wasn't shown at the Salon, the public would never get a chance to see it. The Salon was the official gallery where wealthy buyers purchased artwork. It was the place for people to see what the best artists were doing. (See the previous chapter for more details.) Six years after Monet came to Paris it finally happened. Two of his landscapes were accepted by the Salon. Over the next years the Salon would accept a few more of his paintings, but only those done in a more traditional style.

Even though he was occasionally acknowledged by the Salon, Monet still had a hard time earning a living, and his savings had long since run out. Sometimes artist friends, such as Frédéric Bazille, would buy one of his paintings. This helped Monet pay his bills, at least temporarily.

But whatever money he received from his father or made by selling his work, he spent much more. Monet was good at spending money. He always dressed like a millionaire, even if he had no food to eat. Monet wasn't shy about asking his friends for help. Bazille came from a wealthy family and could afford to help, Monet thought.

To make matters worse, Monet's father finally decided to cut off his son's small allowance. He'd been suspicious of Monet's art education for some time, but now his son had gone too far. His father found out that Monet was living with his girlfriend, Camille. He told Monet to make a decision: marry Camille or else break up. When Monet refused both choices his father cut off his support.

Life with Camille

Monet painted his first picture of Camille Doncieux in 1865, when she was 19. She was the daughter of a well-off merchant whose family lived near Monet's studio. Against her family's wishes, Camille moved out of their home and into Monet's. Two years later they had a son, who they named Jean. Monet loved to paint Jean. You see this little boy in many of his paintings.

Monet was very happy with his new family, but it was extra work to feed them. Renoir, who was also broke, lived nearby with his parents. He brought his friends bread from his family's table to

CLAUDE MONET

London, The Houses of Parliament: Stormy Sky
1904

keep them from starving. Often the Monets had to move because they couldn't pay the rent. Whenever this happened, Monet had to leave behind his paintings as a guarantee to his landlord that he'd pay when he could.

When Jean was three years old, Monet and Camille decided to marry. They hoped their marriage would move Camille's parents to help them out of their financial mess. The small sum they received did help a little. But soon they were faced with another dilemma. Three months after their wedding, war broke out between France and Prussia. Monet didn't want to be drafted again, and he decided to wait out the war in England. He sent his family to live with Boudin, safely away from the fighting, then boarded a ship for the short trip across the English Channel. Monet lived in London for less than a year, but it was an important year in his career.

Fog and Fame

Even though he couldn't speak English, Monet made many discoveries in London. The city's foggy weather and wonderful museums filled him with new ideas about painting. Monet loved London's fog. He painted foggy scenes at all times of the day. When he wasn't painting, he visited London's art museums. He especially liked the artwork of John Constable and J. M. W. Turner, two English artists who painted landscapes. Most important, Monet met Paul Durand-Ruel. Durand-Ruel was a wealthy art dealer from Paris who had also moved to England during the war. While living in London, he opened a gallery there. He was an insightful businessman and was looking to buy paintings done in more modern styles. Durand-Ruel became Monet's savior; he bought several of his paintings. Almost as important, he showed respect for Monet's work, giving him moral support to continue.

Giving Up the Salon

Monet returned to France full of excitement. For once, he had a bit of money. His work was appreciated by Durand-Ruel, so he had more confidence. Monet and his family moved into a house in Argenteuil, a small town near Paris. The house was close to the River Seine—an area full of wonderful scenes to paint. Working quickly, Monet captured impressions of the tugboats and yachts as they floated past.

Monet also enjoyed gardening. He planted a colorful garden and spent many happy hours painting in it. His little son Jean can be seen playing in these garden scenes.

Luckily, Monet was able to sell some of these paintings without the aid of the Salon. His buyers were other painters who recognized his talent, and his dealer Durand-Ruel. Still, he wasn't known out-

CLAUDE MONET

The Artist's Garden at Vetheuil

1881

side of his small circle. He tried to get the Salon to accept more of his work. But he painted in the style that he believed in, and so the answer was always the same: rejected.

Eventually, Monet learned his lesson about the Salon. He would never convince the jury to admire his painting style. He and other artists decided to hold their own exhibit.

On April 15, 1874, the doors opened to their First Exhibition. The critics thought the paintings were horrible. Monet's painting *Impression, Sunrise* especially outraged them.

After the Exhibition

Monet's life had its ups and downs after that dismal First Exhibition. The critics' harsh opinions hurt his feelings. (He would have to endure the same opinions for the next four Impressionist Exhibitions.) Even worse, his finances were once again a mess. In a letter to his good friend Édouard Manet he wrote, "My color-box will stay closed for a long time now, if I can't get out of this mess." Manet always helped with both money and encouragement.

Life looked a little better to Monet when he heard that someone finally bought *Impression: Sunrise* for 800 francs. This was not a very large amount of money, but the wealthy man and his family who bought it would become an important part of Monet's life.

The buyer's name was Ernest Hoschedé, and he owned an exclusive department store in Paris. Hoschedé and his wife, Alice, invited Monet to live in their new mansion while painting murals to help decorate it. During this time Monet and Alice became good friends. But he missed Camille and Jean. He wrote to them often during the months he stayed with the Hoschedés and their five children.

MONET AND MANET

Two artists with such similar names were bound to cause confusion. "Who is this Monet whose name sounds just like mine and who is taking advantage of my notoriety?" Manet asked before he met Monet. They shared other similarities, too. Both artists fought against the stale traditional styles that were promoted by the Salon. But Manet thought the battle should be fought at the Salon. (Which he certainly demonstrated with his painting of a naked picnicker, *Le Déjeuner sur l'Herbe*.) Although Manet never showed his work at an Impressionist Exhibition, he was one of the greatest supporters of the artists who did. Once they met, Manet and Monet became good friends.

Activity

Monet's Garden

When Monet wasn't painting, you would probably find him outside working on his garden. He planted a garden wherever he lived. In his picture The Artist's Garden at Vetheuil, *the shimmering sunflowers seem to be taking over the house.*

Materials

Old magazines or seed catalogs
Scissors
White glue
Water
Small bowl
Flower pot
Potting soil
Flower seeds or bulbs

1. Cut out several pictures of flowers from magazines.

2. Mix equal amounts of glue and water in a bowl. Dip one cut-out picture into the glue solution, covering it entirely. Place it on the side of the flowerpot, smoothing down the edges. Repeat for the remaining cut-out pictures, slightly overlapping each piece. Let dry.

3. Fill the flowerpot with soil, plant a few flower seeds, and add water. Place your pot in a sunny spot and watch your garden bloom.

Years later, Ernest lost all his money and abandoned Alice and the children. To make matters worse, Alice was about to have another baby. Now it was Monet's time to help out. He invited Alice and her children to live with him, Camille, Jean, and their new baby, Michel. Michel's birth had been very hard on Camille and left her extremely weak and in pain. Alice devotedly nursed Camille, but she never recovered. She died when Michel was just one year old. It was a very sad time for Monet. For a long time after, he couldn't paint. He couldn't do anything. But Alice and their household of eight children helped him through these sad days. Over time, Monet became devoted to Alice. She loved him, too, but they couldn't get married because Alice was still married to Ernest. In those days, it was very uncommon to get divorced. Years later, when Ernest died, Monet and Alice did marry.

Success at Last

Gradually, the world began to love Monet's paintings. But the years up until then had been hard on him. After his continued failure in the first four Impressionist Exhibitions, Monet didn't even try to show his work at the fifth and sixth shows. At the Seventh Impressionist Exhibition, Monet tried again with 35 paintings. This time he was a huge success! And across the ocean Americans flocked to see an exhibition of the Paris Impressionists that was held in New York. The public had finally accepted Impressionism.

Life in Giverny

Sixteen years after the First Impressionist Exhibition, Monet would see a dream come true. He was 50 years old and becoming a wealthy man. His dream was to own a big pink stucco house

CLAUDE MONET
The Luncheon
c. 1874

The Fourth Impressionist Exhibition was held four months before Camille's death. In the exhibit, Monet showed 29 paintings. Once again the critics were unimpressed with his "unfinished" style. One reviewer wrote that Monet must have painted all 29 pictures in one afternoon. Luckily, a fellow artist felt differently. Her name was Mary Cassatt, an American whose work was also in the exhibition. She bought one of Monet's paintings for $300. The money helped pay for Camille's medicine and doctor.

with green shutters in the French countryside. Alice, Monet, and their eight children had moved into this house as renters seven years earlier. Now Monet could afford to buy it. He named it after the small village it was near—Giverny (je-ver-NEE).

Of course Monet had to have a garden! He once said that all he was good for was painting and gardening. He filled the area around his house with flowers of every color. At Giverny, Monet's art changed. Up until then, he usually painted everyday slices of modern life. Now, paintings of sailboats and people relaxing at the beach no longer interested him. He was obsessed by the sunlight dancing across natural scenes, like his garden.

CLAUDE MONET
Pool of Water Lilies
1900

But Monet still loved to paint water scenes, so he created a water garden, too. He purchased a nearby meadow that had a stream running through it and built a beautiful pond. With the help of six gardeners, he shaped the meadow into a garden of weeping willows, irises, and water lilies. Building the pond had its problems, though. To make it as large as Monet wished, he had to dig ditches to bring in water from the nearby river. His

neighbors, who were farmers, also used the river and were afraid that Monet might cut off their water supply. Worse yet, they thought his exotic plants might pollute the water, poisoning their cattle, who drank downstream. Monet had to convince the town council to allow him to build his pond.

After his pond was complete Monet added a finishing touch. It was the most beautiful part of his water garden—an arched wooden bridge. Everyone called it the *Japanese Bridge*.

Haystacks

The countryside around Giverny was filled with beautiful fields and dense woods. Monet hiked through the area around his home, hunting for new impressions to paint. Often, his stepdaughter Blanche would join him.

One day a large haystack in a nearby farm caught his attention. Monet set up his easel and started to paint. As he painted, the sun changed position. New colors came alive, and the shadows shifted. Monet sent Blanche back to the house for a new canvas. He captured this impression, then sent Blanche back, again and again. Monet was obsessed by the changing light. He went back to the same field, at all times of the year. Blanche was in charge of a wheelbarrow full of canvases. When

winter came, the farmer who owned the field was ready to remove the haystacks. He needed them to feed his cows! Monet paid him to leave the haystacks alone. Some of his favorite scenes were painted that winter in the snow.

When 15 of his haystack paintings were exhibited together in Paris, every single one was sold within three days. It was amazing to see them together, at one time. One critic called Monet a poet.

Painting at Giverny

Monet realized that the most beautiful scenes he could imagine were right outside his door, in his garden. That's where he could be found during the last 20 years of his life.

At times his old artist friends, such as Renoir and Cézanne, would visit Giverny. After a lavish lunch in his cheery yellow dining room, Monet would proudly take them on a tour of his water garden. Sometimes they would set up their easels, as in the old days, and paint together.

Young artists from America flocked to Giverny, too. They wanted to learn about Impressionism from the master. This drove Monet crazy—he wanted to be left alone to paint. The young artists had to be satisfied with living in the same village as their hero. They created an artist's colony down the road from the pink house. One American

CLAUDE MONET
Haystack in Winter
1890–91

painter, Theodore Butler, was luckier than the others. Monet's stepdaughter Suzanne fell in love with him and married him.

Monet seldom left his home and garden. He painted many versions of his Japanese bridge. His favorite subjects were the water lilies that floated in his pond. He still painted trees and clouds, but now they only appeared as reflections in the water.

When Monet was 76 years old he decided to paint a series of enormous water lily murals. They were over 6 feet high and up to 55 feet long. These murals would cover the walls of two large oval rooms. He built a special studio to paint them in. By now, the images of water lilies were so etched

Mini Haystack and Field

Monet could paint the same thing again and again, even a simple pile of hay. His picture Haystack in Winter *shows the colors of the sun as they bounce off a snowy field. Monet's snow is blue—the color of the reflected sky. If you ever see snow on a bright, clear day, you'll notice that it does look blue.*

Materials

Pencil
Coffee mug
2 pieces white construction paper,
   8 inches x 10 inches (20 cm x 25 cm)
Scissors

Ruler
Crayons
Clear plastic tape
Flashlight

CLAUDE MONET

Detail from *Haystack in Winter*

1. Trace the bottom of a coffee mug onto one piece of construction paper. Cut out the circle shape. Cut a slot from the edge of the circle to its center.

2. From the same piece of paper, cut a strip 2 inches by 8 inches (5 cm by 20 cm). Notice the colors that Monet used to paint his haystack. Color the circle and strip using similar colors.

3. Form the circle into a pointed hat shape and tape. Form the strip of paper into a ring that fits under the hat shape. Tape them together. Set aside.

4. Place the second piece of paper so that its 8-inch (20 cm) edge is at the bottom and top. Draw a line 4 inches (10 cm) from the top. This is where the field meets the woods. Fold the top toward you, along this line. Color a snow scene using Monet's colors. Tape the haystack onto the base art.

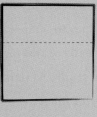

5. Use the flashlight to see how the shadow of the haystack changes as you hold it at different angles around the stack. This is how the sun lit up Monet's real haystack during the months he painted it. When you find an angle you like, trace its shape with a pencil. Color the shadow using the complementary colors of the haystack just as Monet did. Colors that sit opposite each other on the color wheel are called *complementary colors*. Red and green, yellow and purple, and blue and orange are pairs of complementary colors. Monet often painted a shadow using the complementary color of the object that cast the shadow.

Another Impression: Find your own haystack to paint at different times of the day. Your version might be the tree outside your window or a building you can see from your window. Make two or more colored drawings of it at different times of the day. Notice how its shadow and colors change depending on the sunlight.

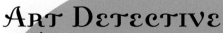

Art Detective

How to Spot a Monet

Here are some characteristics that help distinguish Monet's work:

- **Light!** Monet wanted to capture the light. He paid more attention to how the light hit his subject than the subject itself.
- **Landscapes!** If people are in the scene, they are often mere blurs.
- **Water!** It didn't matter what type of water—oceans, lakes, rivers, or ponds. They all made great mirrors for reflecting the sky, trees, and boats.
- **Young woman with a little boy.** Monet's wife Camille and their son Jean were Monet's favorite subjects in his early paintings.
- **Water lilies!** Monet spent his last 20 years painting water lilies.

upon his mind he could paint them in a studio from memory. It was fortunate that Monet could rely on his memory because he was losing his eyesight to cataracts. (Cataracts make it seem as if you are looking through a hazy yellow film.) Many of Monet's paintings from this time do appear more yellow. Finally, Monet had an operation on his eyes. It was a success. He was so happy to see the clear, bright world again! At age 84 he said, "I'm working as never before, happy with what I'm doing. . . . I only ask to live to a hundred."

Monet was able to finish his water lily murals before he died at age 86. Today, they line the oval walls in a museum in Paris called the Orangerie.

Monet and the World Today

Fifty-four years after his death, Monet's home and beautiful garden were opened as a museum. Today visitors from all over the world flock to Giverny, looking to capture their own impressions. While in Paris, they visit his water lily murals at the Musée de l'Orangerie. Artists have compared the Orangerie to another famous site left to us by Michelangelo. They call the room filled with Monet's murals the Sistine Chapel of modern art. It's said that these large shimmering canvases of color and light were the starting point for a style of painting called abstract art.

CLAUDE MONET

Water Lilies

1906

Activity

Paper Water Lily

Monet spent many creative years painting the water lilies that floated in his water garden at Giverny. He was fascinated by the light bouncing off the water.

Materials

Pink, yellow, and green construction paper	1 nickel
Ruler	Paints, any type
Pencil	Paintbrush
Scissors	Glue stick
1 quarter	Optional: Water
	Blue food coloring

1. Cut 3 pieces of pink paper into 6-inch (15 cm) squares. Cut 3 pieces of yellow paper into 3-inch squares (7.5 cm). Cut 1 piece of green paper into the shape of a lily pad.

2. Place a quarter in the center of a pink square and trace around it with a pencil. Draw 8 petals around the circle, to the outer edge of the paper. Stack all 3 pieces of pink paper, with the drawn sheet on top. Cut out the pattern.

3. Repeat step 2 using the yellow squares, tracing a nickel at the center.

4. Add splashes of color to make the petals look like an Impressionist painting. Paint the pink petals with dabs of orange, purple, and rose. Add orange and yellow-orange to the yellow petals. Let dry.

5. Crease each petal down its center and fold it upward at its base. Set 1 yellow piece aside. Apply glue to the center of all the other pieces. Stack them together, with the pink pieces on the bottom. Fan out the layers so you can see all the petals. Finish with the unglued (yellow) piece on top. Glue all on top of the green lily pad.

Another Impression: Glue a small plastic lid to the bottom of the lily pad and float it in a bowl of water. Color the water with a few drops of food coloring. Or use your lily in place of a bow to decorate a gift.

PIERRE AUGUSTE RENOIR

The Umbrellas

1881–85

Pierre Auguste Renoir

While young Claude Monet was exploring the cliffs near his home in Le Havre, another little boy was playing in the streets of Paris. One day they would meet at art school and become best friends. The boy's name was Pierre Auguste Renoir.

Pierre Auguste Renoir was born in Limoges, France, on February 25, 1841. When Renoir was four years old, his family moved to Paris. They rented a small apartment very near the palace of King Louis-Philippe and his wife, Queen Marie Amélie. Even though Pierre Auguste had the King and Queen as neighbors, his family didn't live in luxury. The Renoirs were poor. Their apartment was so small that Pierre Auguste, who had four brothers and sisters, had to sleep on his father's workbench. His father was a tailor, and worked at home making men's suits. His mother was a seamstress. Young Renoir didn't mind sleeping on a hard bench, but he didn't like the lost pins on the floor that always poked him when he forgot to wear his slippers.

Living next to the palace was great! The courtyard made a terrific playground for Renoir and his friends. Their favorite game was cops and robbers. It was a noisy game and often drew the attention of the royal residents of the palace. When this happened, a window in the palace would open and an elegant lady-in-waiting would motion to the children to quiet down. Whenever Renoir and his friends saw her, they gathered under her window like baby birds waiting to be fed. Then another woman would appear and throw candy down to them. She was the Queen, Marie Amélie.

Even when he was very little, Renoir loved to draw. Drawing paper was scarce in the Renoir household, but that didn't stop him. Instead, he used his father's tailor's chalk and drew pictures on

the floor of the apartment. His father was annoyed when he couldn't find his chalk, but he thought the drawings were pretty good. "Auguste will do something some day," his mother predicted. "He's got the eye for it."

Renoir also had musical talent, and he sang solos in his church's choir. One day, when he was 13 years old, the choirmaster went to see his parents. He wanted to give young Renoir a complete musical education. He even promised him a job singing in the opera chorus. The offer was tempting because Renoir loved to sing and it was time for him to learn a trade. Back then, children of working-class parents didn't go to high school or college. It was assumed that they would start earning a living at a young age. Renoir was old enough now to help support his family. But he was very shy and horrified to think about performing in front of so many people. If it were his only offer, he would have accepted it. Luckily, Renoir had another job offer that was perfect for him.

The Beginning of a Career

The owner of a porcelain factory had heard about Renoir's talent as an artist. He needed someone to paint decorations on plates, cups, and vases and offered to take Renoir on as an apprentice. His father was very proud of being from Limoges, a city famous for its porcelain, so it wasn't hard for Renoir to make the choice.

He became a porcelain painter. At first he painted decorative flowers around the borders of the china. It wasn't long before he was promoted to painting portraits of famous people on the pieces. One of the most popular portraits was of Marie Antoinette, the former Queen of France. She was notorious because of her bad luck, being beheaded on the guillotine 60 years earlier. Renoir painted her image so many times that he could have done it with his eyes closed. To make things more interesting, he started giving her a cute little nose instead of the long pointed one she really had. This would have gotten most painters fired, but not Renoir. He was too good an artist, and he actually made a very good salary until a machine was invented that could stamp Queen Marie Antoinette's portrait on the porcelain pieces. The machine was faster and painted the correct size nose every time. Renoir was replaced by a machine at the age of 17.

For the next three years, Renoir found other painting jobs. Many café owners hired him to paint murals on the walls of their restaurants. During his free time, he visited art museums to see the works of the famous masters. He especially liked the work of Jean Honoré Fragonard, a French artist who lived a hundred years earlier and painted in a style called Rococo. When Renoir was 20 years old he decided to study seriously with a well-known artist named Charles Gleyre.

Gleyre taught his students to paint and draw as the Old Masters had done. The tones were dark, brush strokes smooth, and poses formal. It was all very serious work. Renoir worked hard but was always very cheerful. His cheerfulness showed in the way he painted. Gleyre once looked at what Renoir was drawing and said, "Young man, you are very skillful, very gifted, but no doubt you took up painting just to amuse yourself." The last part wasn't a compliment! Renoir replied, "Certainly. If it didn't amuse me I wouldn't be doing it." Renoir had a few of his own ideas about painting.

Meeting Monet

One day a new student joined Gleyre's studio. His name was Claude Monet. Unlike Renoir, who was rather shy, Monet made sure he was noticed. Right away he refused to sit on a stool while painting. "Only fit for milking cows," he announced. One day Monet decided that he would set up his easel on the platform where the teacher usually stood. This didn't win him any points with the master. What impressed Renoir the most about Monet was his worldly manner. Renoir was very modest about the type of clothes he wore but was delighted with the

spectacular elegance of Monet. About his new friend he said, "He was penniless and he wore shirts with lace at the cuffs!"

Renoir and Monet became very good friends. With a few others, they finally left Gleyre's studio to pursue their own ideas about painting. Monet invited his fellow rebel painters to paint with him in the nearby forest of Fontainebleau. There they would set up their easels and paint pictures of nature. Renoir was usually so absorbed in his subject that he didn't notice anything else around him. One day Monet asked him for something, but didn't get an answer. Monet had to reach into Renoir's shirt pocket to get it himself. Renoir finally noticed when Monet's bushy beard tickled his face. He was so still when he worked that the deer would come out of the woods and stand next to him, watching him paint. After he noticed the deer, he started bringing them bread to eat. Big mistake! Now the deer nuzzled against him as he tried to paint, and he couldn't get anything done.

Monet and Renoir shared an apartment, which was also their art studio. They managed to make a living by painting portraits of local tradespeople. When they couldn't get money, they swapped their work for food or clothing. Monet was a great salesman and had a knack for getting customers. Renoir did beautiful portraits, and people enjoyed posing for him. He charmed them with his cheerful

RENOIR'S METHODS

Renoir thought paintings should be "likable, joyous, and pretty." He said, "There are enough unpleasant things in this world. We don't have to paint them as well." It is this joy of life that sets his paintings apart from those of the other Impressionists. His favorite subjects were young women, children, and scenes of Parisians out enjoying life. Renoir used thinned paint for his skin tones, applying it with feathery, comma-shaped brush strokes. As he added other elements to the painting he applied his strokes more freely, using thicker paint and choppier strokes. His outdoor scenes are dappled with many colors, creating a dance of shadow and sunlight.

Renoir traveled to Italy when he was 40 years old. While in Italy the paintings of the Old Masters, such as Michelangelo, influenced him. When he returned home his painting style became smoother and his shapes were more clearly defined. He combined this style of painting with the light and bright colors of Impressionism.

personality. But not all his customers were easy to please. "I remember especially the portrait of a cobbler's wife, which I painted in exchange for a pair of shoes," recalled Renoir. "Every time I thought the picture was finished and saw myself wearing the shoes, along came the aunt, the daughter, and even the old servant, to criticize."

All the money the two friends could scrape together went to pay for their studio, a model, a sack of beans, and coal for their stove. To save money, they only lit their stove to keep the model warm while she was posing. They set their beans to cook as soon as she got there.

Renoir dreamed of getting one of his paintings accepted by the Salon. In 1863 he got his wish. Later, a few more paintings were also accepted, but only because he did them in a more traditional style. The fresh, colorful, exciting style of painting that he preferred would never be accepted by the judges.

Making an Impression

In 1874 Renoir exhibited this style at the First Impressionist Exhibition. Renoir couldn't wait to find out what the public would think of his paintings. What he found is that most people didn't like the new works at all. They thought his paintings looked unfinished and sloppy. One critic diagnosed Renoir's style as madness. What really upset Renoir was that the critics didn't even mention him in their articles. It was as if he weren't important enough. Still, people knew that he was one of the rebels. Soon even his small portrait painting business suffered. No one wanted to be painted by "one of the lunatics."

Luckily, Renoir had a second talent to fall back on—his charm. A small group of influential friends decided on a plan: if they could convince a few of the wealthy society ladies to have their portraits painted by Renoir, others would follow. This group of admirers thought that Renoir's charm, and the way he made women look so beautiful, would win these wealthy women over. They knew that these ladies were not art critics and wouldn't be swayed by what others thought was acceptable art.

They went straight to the top and approached Marguerite Charpentier, the wife of a wealthy publisher. They convinced her that she ought to have her portrait done. It turned out to be a masterpiece! As planned, all of her friends insisted that Renoir paint their portraits, too. Charpentier's influence was so great that she succeeded in showing her portrait at the next Salon. She wasn't satisfied with showing it in her own home; it should be admired by the whole world! She got her way, and Renoir was launched on the path to fame.

ABOUT THE PICTURE

The Umbrellas, 1881–85

If you look closely at Renoir's famous painting *The Umbrellas*, you can see how his painting style changed after he visited Italy. He worked on *The Umbrellas* for many years before it was finished.

Renoir painted the woman and two girls on the right first. They're done in the Impressionist style, with quick, feathery brush strokes. He finished the painting four years later. By then Renoir used smoother brush strokes. You can see his new style when you look at the man and woman on the left. Their shapes have a more solid outline, too.

Another way we know that this painting was worked on over a span of time is by looking at the women's dresses. Renoir always dressed his models in the latest fashion. When he began *The Umbrellas*, women wore hats and frilly dresses. A few years later, simpler dresses were in style, and women had stopped wearing hats.

PIERRE AUGUSTE RENOIR
Details from *The Umbrellas*
1881–85

How to Draw a Face

Renoir's favorite thing to paint was portraits. It's easy to draw a face once you know a few tricks. Practice with a simple drawing, then try making a self-portrait.

Materials

Paper
Pencil
Ruler

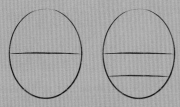

1. Draw a large oval, then draw a line dividing it in half, so there is a top and a bottom.

2. Draw a line halfway between the line you drew in step 1 and the bottom of the oval.

3. Draw a line halfway between the line you drew in step 2 and the bottom of the oval.

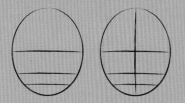

4. Draw a line going up and down, dividing the oval in half, so there is a left and right half.

5. Using the lines as guide, draw eyes, nose, and mouth in their correct place, as shown. Each eye should be halfway between the center guide and the side of the oval. The mouth is as wide as the distance from the center of each eye. The nose is centered.

6. Add hair, ears, and any other details you'd like. Erase the guidelines.

Another Impression: Once you've practiced drawing a simple face, try drawing one that looks like you. Look into a mirror and make the features on the face match your own. Look carefully at the shape of your face. It may not be exactly shaped like an oval. If it isn't, start your picture by drawing a shape that's more like your own face.

50

PIERRE AUGUSTE RENOIR

Detail from *Portraits of Children (the children of Martial Caillebotte)*

Renoir enjoyed painting portraits of beautiful women and children. He also worked on larger scenes of outdoor cafés and restaurants. These pictures are filled with groups of people out having a good time.

Before painting a café scene, Renoir would visit the café several times to study it. He watched how the late afternoon sun shone through the foliage, dappling the dancers in light and shadow. As it got darker, he noticed how the lanterns glowed in the twilight. Renoir spent many evenings enjoying the mood of the merrymakers as they laughed and flirted on warm summer nights. When he felt ready, he brought his large canvas and paints and set up his easel. Renoir made friends easily, and the local people enjoyed seeing him at the café. In his gray striped suit, flowing blue tie with white polka dots, and little round felt hat, he became a familiar sight at the outdoor cafés.

Family Life

One day, while Renoir was having dinner at a local restaurant, he spotted his perfect model. She had a cute little nose, just like his version of Marie

PIERRE AUGUSTE RENOIR
Detail from *The Ball at the Moulin de la Galette*
1876

PIERRE AUGUSTE RENOIR

Portraits of Children (the children of Martial Caillebotte)

1895

Antoinette! He was 38 years old, and she was 20. Her name was Aline Charigot and she worked as a seamstress—just like Renoir's mother. Aline was cheerful and down-to-earth, a country girl from a family of wine growers. A romance began.

Eventually Renoir and Aline decided to live together, much to the regret of Aline's mother, who was against her daughter's relationship with her "penniless sweetheart." Renoir didn't propose to Aline for several years because he felt uncertain he'd be able to support her and any children they might have. He didn't want a wife "who went out to work." In Renoir's time it was common for married women to be homemakers. Still, Renoir's opinions about the role of women were a bit extreme. "I like women best when they don't know how to read," he once remarked. There was no doubt that he adored Aline. A friend who had observed Renoir painting her picture recalled, "There were times when he would put down his palette and gaze at her instead of painting, asking himself why he tried, since what he was trying to achieve was there already."

Eleven years after they met, Renoir and Aline were married. Meanwhile, they had a son, and two more followed after their marriage. One of their sons, Jean Renoir, grew up to be a famous movie director. Renoir was a proud father with definite theories about raising children. He believed that young eyes should be exposed only to cheerfully

painted walls, pretty colors, and simple, natural things like flowers and fruit. Always worried about the children's safety, he made certain that their house was child-proofed. Renoir even rounded off the corners of the tables and marble mantelpieces in their home to prevent injuries. To help with the children, Aline's young cousin Gabrielle came to live with them. Many of Renoir's paintings are of his wife, young sons, and Gabrielle. It was a joyful time for Renoir; he loved his family and his art-work was finally selling.

Recycling Renoir

Along with being part of the family, Gabrielle became one of Renoir's favorite models and assis-tants. Renoir never forced his little boys to sit still and pose for him. Gabrielle would interest them with a game or a book long enough for their father to paint them. Often, when Gabrielle modeled for him, she would start a fire in the stove to keep warm. Sometimes Renoir insisted that she use his paintings to light the fire instead of newspaper. These were studies that Renoir thought were not good enough to save. Even though he kept a close watch on her, Gabrielle was able to hide a painting or two before it hit the flames. She couldn't bear the thought of a Renoir being destroyed. On the other hand, Renoir's brother-in-law wasn't so concerned. During a visit to their home in the country, Renoir asked his sister and her husband to store several canvases he had painted while visiting. When he came back to get them, he found that they had been used to repair a hole in the roof and to cover a rabbit hutch. Renoir's brother-in-law didn't think it was a big deal; the artist could just paint a few new ones. "What difference does it make to Renoir?" he asked. "He paints that stuff for the fun of it."

A Home in the South

When he was 57 years old, Renoir began suffering from rheumatism. This disease causes stiffness and pain in muscles and joints, and it attacked Renoir's hands. Later, he and his family moved to Cagnes, in the south of France, where they hoped the warm dry climate would ease his aches and pains. They bought a beautiful farm called Les Collettes and built a house there. Even when he was in pain, Renoir never stopped painting. Toward the end of his life, his hands hurt so badly he couldn't even hold a paintbrush. Instead, he tied the brushes to his hands with strips of cloth. He could no longer walk and was carried in a sedan chair, a portable chair supported by two bamboo poles. Unfortunately, Aline was also ill. She was diagnosed with diabetes, a blood sugar

PIERRE AUGUSTE RENOIR

Dance in the City
1883

PIERRE AUGUSTE RENOIR

The Artist's Son Jean Drawing

1901

disease that left her very tired. The remedy, insulin, had not yet been discovered. When she died of a heart attack at age 56, Renoir was devastated. He would have to face his final years alone.

Renoir died from heart failure at the age of 78. A few months before his death, he learned that the Louvre had bought one of his portraits of Marguerite Charpentier. The museum director invited Renoir to see the painting, and a special visit was arranged. Unable to walk, Renoir was carried through the galleries of the Louvre in his sedan chair, accompanied by the museum curators and a friend. He passed the famous paintings that he had copied as a student, stopping to admire them one last time, and then came upon his own work, the portrait of a woman who 42 years earlier had launched him on the road to fame.

Since the day he decided to become an artist, Renoir practiced painting every day. On the morning of his death he asked for his paintbox and brushes and painted a picture of a vase of flowers.

Remembering Renoir

Two years before Renoir's death, his painting *The Umbrellas* was given to the National Gallery in London. A hundred English artists and collectors signed a letter to Renoir praising him. "From the moment your picture was hung among the famous

Art Detective

How to Spot a Renoir
Here are some characteristics that help distinguish Renoir's work:
- **Portraits!** Look for close-ups of women and children, often in a garden setting.
- **Fat pink cheeks and creamy white skin!** Renoir's favorite models had these features in common.
- **Children!** Paintings of children dressed in their Sunday best.
- **Dancing!** Couples enjoying a twirl on the dance floor.
- **Outdoor gatherings!** Groups of people out having a good time at the local café.

works of the Old Masters, we had the joy of recognizing that one of our contemporaries had taken at once his place among the great masters of European tradition."

During his long life, Renoir created over 6,000 paintings. They hang in museums all over the world. His beautiful portraits, landscapes, and flowers glow with a rainbow of color, reminding us of Renoir's words: "Paintings should be likable, joyous, and pretty."

The restaurant where Renoir painted The Ball at the Moulin de la Galette *was named for a kind of cake they served. Called a* galette, *it resembles a waffle. There are many kinds, but the Galette des Rois is the most fun. Every January 6th, families all over France eat this cake while celebrating Twelfth Night. This holiday, which is 12 days after Christmas, commemorates the coming of the Wise Men to the Christ child.*

A bean is hidden in the galette before it is baked. The fun begins when the cake is served. Whoever gets the piece containing the bean becomes king or queen for the night. He or she wears a crown and everyone must treat that person like royalty.

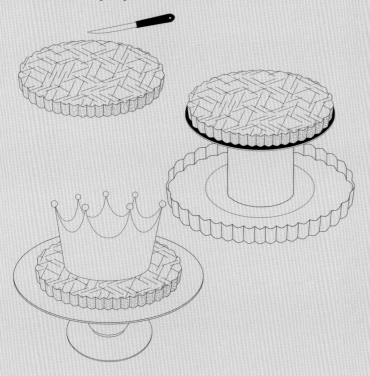

Galette des Rois (Twelfth Night Cake)

8 servings   *Adult help suggested*

Ingredients

4 egg yolks

1 cup plus 3 tablespoons granulated sugar

1⅓ cups unsalted butter, softened but not melted (2 sticks plus 5⅓ tablespoons)

4 cups all-purpose flour, sifted

1 dry bean

Egg Glaze
1 egg
1 teaspoon water
1 teaspoon sugar

Utensils

10 inch fluted metal tart pan with removable bottom

Large mixing bowl

Electric mixer

Large spoon

Small mixing bowl

Fork

Pastry brush

Butter knife

Toothpick

Wide jar

Serving dish

1. Preheat the oven to 375° F. Grease the tart pan and set it aside. Combine the egg yolks and sugar in a bowl and beat with an electric mixer for 4 minutes, until very creamy.

2. Add butter and flour alternately, a little at a time, and beat slowly. The batter will be thick, almost like cookie dough. Add the bean to the mixture. Press the batter into the greased baking pan, flattening the top with the palm of your hand. Batter should be about 1 inch thick.

3. In a small bowl, use a fork to beat the egg with water and sugar to make the glaze. Brush the glaze over the top of the cake. Score lightly with a knife, making a design.

4. Bake at 375° F for 35 to 40 minutes, until an inserted toothpick comes out clean and the top of the cake is golden. Set aside to cool.

5. Ask an adult to help you remove the cake from the pan. Set the bottom of the tart pan on top of a wide jar and gently press on the outside ring until it drops down. Slide the cake off the bottom of the pan and onto a serving dish.

6. Make a crown out of posterboard for the king or queen of the day.

EDGAR DEGAS

Cafe-Concert at the Ambassadeurs

c. 1876–77

Edgar Degas

Edgar Degas had something to say about everything. When it came to the painting methods of the Impressionists, he grumbled, "Don't tell me about those fellows cluttering the fields with their easels . . . the stupid fools." And he didn't like the name "Impressionist" one bit. "I prefer to be called an Independent," he announced to all who would listen. Degas was different from his fellow Impressionists, but he was one of their most loyal members.

Born in Paris on July 19, 1834, Degas was the oldest of five children. His parents had met while living in France, but they had grown up in other countries. His mother was American. Her family owned a cotton exporting business in New Orleans, Louisiana. Degas's father came from a wealthy banking family in Naples, Italy. Unlike many of his artist friends, Degas came from a very wealthy family.

Like most children from wealthy families, Degas was first tutored at home. When he was 12 years old, he was sent to an elite boarding school for boys. Fortunately, his school wasn't far from home. On Sunday mornings, his father would take him on outings in Paris. Degas's father loved art, and they spent many Sundays visiting art museums, especially the Louvre. Edgar especially admired the works of the Old Masters such as Raphael and Rembrandt. Sometimes they would visit one of his father's friends. Several of them collected the paintings of famous artists and enjoyed showing off their treasures to Edgar.

Even though Degas's father loved art, he thought his son should study something more practical, like law. This would prepare him to take over the family business. To please his father, Edgar enrolled in law school. During his free time, he brought his sketch pad to the Louvre and copied the works of the great masters. After his first term of law school, Degas decided to quit. His father realized that he wasn't cut out for law and agreed to send him to art school.

Degas took his art studies very seriously. Shy and moody, he didn't have many friends. He preferred to be alone. Although Degas studied at the studio of a respected teacher, he liked to set up his easel at the Louvre and copy the paintings of the Old Masters. Students often copied famous paintings as a painting exercise. They studied how famous painters of the past used color to create effects, and then tried to imitate them. Copying masterpieces helped aspiring artists develop their skills. If the copies were well done and sold, then students could earn extra money.

Off to Italy

In Degas's time, Paris was considered the artistic capital of the world. It was in Italy, though, where you'd find the most famous Renaissance paintings. The Renaissance, 400 years before Degas, was an incredible time in the history of art. Renaissance painters achieved a natural, lifelike quality in their portraits. This was very different from the flat look found in the Middle Ages, just before the Renaissance. Leonardo da Vinci, Michelangelo, and Raphael are all famous Renaissance artists. After two years of art school, Degas moved to Italy to study the works of these great painters.

While in Florence, Degas met a group of Italian painters called the Macchiaioli, or spot painters. They were given this name because they dabbed spots of contrasting colors on their canvases to show the effects of light and shadow. Just like the Impressionists in France, they met regularly at crowded cafés and loudly challenged the established traditions of art. Of course, the Macchiaioli rebelled against the traditions of Italian art. They preferred to paint scenes of everyday life and landscapes, not the traditional subjects of religious and historical themes. They sounded just like the "lunatics" in Paris. At the time, Degas was following the path of traditional artists. Such revolutionary talk must have amazed him.

During this time, Degas sent some of his work home to his father, but he worried that it was not good enough. His father quickly replied, "I was very pleased and I can tell you, you have taken a tremendous step forward in art. You've no need to torment yourself any more . . . calm down."

Home to Paris

Paris was a hotbed of activity when Degas returned almost three years later. The new emperor, Napoléon III, was tearing down the old slums and building a beautiful modern city. Wealthy Parisians spent their money lavishly on fashionable clothes, tickets to the opera, evenings at the cafés, and art. The official place to buy art, the Salon, was attracting hundreds of thousands of viewers every year.

Degas was now a talented artist who painted traditional themes, and his father was anxious to see his work shown at the Salon. Degas, however, was not as anxious. Because he was wealthy, he didn't have much need to earn money. He would rather clutter his studio with piles of paintings than try to find buyers for them. Gruff and unsociable, Degas became entirely absorbed in his art. "What is fermenting in that head is frightening," his brother René once stated. Finally, six years after his return from Italy, Degas submitted a painting to the Salon. Titled *The Sufferings of the City of New Orleans*, it depicted a battle scene from a medieval war. A large historical scene was just what the judges liked, so it was accepted; unfortunately, it was ignored by the public.

A lot of attention was paid to a painting that hung near Degas's work. "Repulsive!" said one critic. "Ugly!" said another. The painting, titled *Olympia*, was of a naked woman, a subject that had been painted for hundreds of years. This woman was different, though. She was not a goddess floating on a clamshell or a nymph lounging under a tree with a band of chubby cupids. This woman reclined on a couch with a little black cat at her feet. She looked like a modern Parisian. What's more, she was staring right out at her audience! Scandalous! Once again, Édouard Manet had created an uproar with one of his paintings.

Becoming an Impressionist

Degas had first met Manet three years earlier, while copying a painting at the Louvre. Manet thought Degas's copy was pretty good and said so. Degas came to learn that Manet was a tremendous artist himself. This became even more obvious when Degas saw *Olympia*. When Degas compared his traditional, old-fashioned style to the fresh, modern style of Manet, he started to think differently about his own work.

The two artists soon became friends. Manet brought Degas to meet other new-thinking artists at their neighborhood hangout—the Café Guerbois. He met the cheery Renoir, big-talking Monet, and many other rebellious painters and writers. The group welcomed the fashionably

EDGAR DEGAS

Blue Dancers

1897

dressed Degas, who was never seen without his silk top hat, gloves, and walking cane. But they soon realized he had a sharp, biting tongue. You didn't want to disagree with him too often for fear of his caustic remarks. His sarcastic wit could be entertaining, though, as long as someone else was the target. Even though the hot-tempered Degas didn't agree with everything that was said at these boisterous gatherings, his artwork would never be the same. Degas, however, had his own ideas about what the new modern art should look like.

Degas's Methods

Degas didn't think of himself as an Impressionist and deeply resented being regarded as one. Of all the painters of the Impressionist circle, he was least impressed with Monet. There was an incident when the two artists happened to meet at a gallery that was showing Monet's work. "Let me get out of here!" Degas tactlessly burst out, "Those reflections in the water hurt my eyes!"

Unlike his fellow Impressionists, Degas preferred painting indoor scenes. A singer at a café or a group of young ballerinas in a dance studio interested him much more than sailboats and flowerpots. While Monet and his pals worked outdoors, at the scene, Degas worked in his studio, painting from memory and sketches. He thought that when

EDGAR DEGAS
Detail from *Blue Dancers*
1897

PIERRE AUGUSTE RENOIR
Detail from *The Ball at the Moulin de la Galette*
1876

you worked from memory you painted "only what has struck you, what is essential."

Their ideas about technique differed, too. Most of the Impressionists filled their canvases with spontaneous dabs of paint. Degas was controlled and methodical. He used what he learned from the Old Masters, concentrating on careful drawing. He used lines to form the image he was painting. In his pastel *Blue Dancers*, for example, Degas used dark lines to define the shape of the dancers' arms. Most Impressionists didn't believe in using lines. Instead they used colorful shapes to form their images. For example, in *The Ball at Moulin de la Galette*, Renoir defined the shape of his dancers with small patches of color.

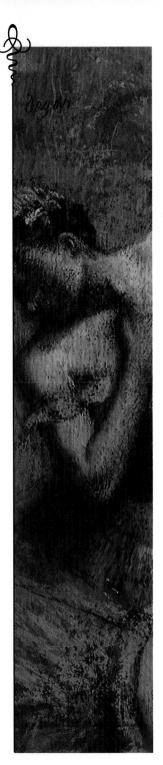

Degas did share the philosophy of the Impressionists, however—that the traditional themes had to be changed. He painted scenes of everyday life in Paris. But Degas looked in very different places for his scenes. Nothing escaped his critical eye, from the liveliest café-concert singer to the dreariest laundry woman. Degas captured these scenes of modern-day Paris in his sketchbooks, then worked up finished pictures in oil or pastel in his studio.

The First Impressionist Exhibit

In 1874, the year of the First Impressionist Exhibition, Degas was 40 years old. Earlier in that year, his father had died suddenly. It was only then that Degas learned his family was nearly bankrupt. For the first time in his life, he was forced to sell his paintings.

Even though the exhibit was a disaster for the Impressionists as a whole, Degas managed to sell 7 of the 10 paintings he exhibited. His meticulous drawing and painting techniques appealed to some art collectors. His artwork wasn't like those "messy canvases which were slapped together" by Monet and Renoir.

No matter how much he needed the money, Degas never liked selling his paintings. He couldn't

JAPANESE PRINTS

Before the 1850s, Japanese art was unfamiliar in France. Woodblock prints, known as Ukiyo-e ("images of the floating world"), caused a lot of excitement when they finally arrived. They influenced the Impressionists who collected them. Their striking designs included unusual viewpoints and the "cut off at the edge" effect of a snapshot. This type of composition was very different from traditional European art. Experiencing a Paris exhibit of this work would affect the work of Degas and Mary Cassatt.

part with his work. He never thought they were good enough. Once he told a friend, "I would like to be rich enough to buy back all my pictures and destroy them by pushing my foot through the canvas."

But people did buy his work. One year after the First Impressionist Exhibition, a young woman brought her friend into a gallery and showed her a pastel of a ballet rehearsal done by Degas. The young woman was an artist from America named Mary Cassatt. Her friend was Louise Elder. "I scarcely knew how to appreciate it," Louise said, "or whether I liked it or not, for I believe it takes special brain cells to understand Degas. There was nothing the matter with Miss Cassatt's brain cells, however, and she left me in no doubt as to the desirability of the purchase and I bought it on her advice."

It would be two years before Cassatt actually met Degas, but she was a fan of his work long before they met. "I used to go and flatten my nose against the window and absorb all I could of his art," Cassatt remembered. "It changed my life." Imagine her excitement the day he walked into her studio, introduced himself, and asked her to join in the Impressionist Exhibitions. Degas and Cassatt developed a warm friendship. In her own way, however, Cassatt could be as brutally frank as Degas about art. There were times when they disagreed so intensely that neither would speak to the other for weeks.

Painting Ballerinas

Dancers were Degas's favorite subject. Ballets were very popular in Paris. Young girls dreamed of becoming famous ballerinas. It was hard work and not very glamorous. The young girls weren't even called students—they were called rats.

Degas understood how hard the girls worked. "When people talk of ballet dancers," he explained, "they imagine them covered with jewelry and lav-

ishly maintained with a mansion, carriage, and servants, just as it says in storybooks. In reality more of them are poor girls doing a very demanding job and finding it hard to make ends meet."

He spent hours watching the young girls practice at the dance studio. Degas was fascinated by their gauzy costumes and the movement of their bodies as they twirled and leaped across the floor. He painted many of his ballerina scenes with pastels, a chalk-like crayon. With pastels, he could work more quickly than with oils. They didn't need time to dry, and the colors were very bright.

Degas also showed the dancers resting. In some paintings, they waited on the sidelines, adjusted their costumes, yawned, and scratched their backs. This outraged the critics. They were used to seeing only "beautiful" portraits of famous ballerinas. Degas's portrayals were disturbing. But he didn't care what critics said; he recorded the scenes as he saw them.

Degas even made sculptures of ballerinas. He exhibited one of them at the Sixth Impressionist Exhibition in 1881. *Little Dancer of Fourteen Years* was 38 inches tall and made of red wax. He dressed her in real dance slippers, a gauze tutu, and a silk bodice. He made her hair using horsehair, and tied it back with a satin bow. In 1881 no one put real clothes and hair on a sculpture. The visitors at the exhibit were shocked.

Watering Can Caution

Whenever Degas came across one of his paintings that someone had bought, he would want to make changes to it. One pastel that disturbed him was owned by his friend Henri Rouart. After seeing it again and again whenever he came to visit, Degas finally persuaded Rouart to let him take it back for corrections. Rouart was very fond of the pastel, but Degas wore him out with his persistence. After some time, his friend asked Degas about his beloved pastel. But the artist always put him off with one excuse or another. Finally Degas had to confess that his little retouch had become a disaster and the pastel was completely destroyed. To make up for the loss, Degas gave Rouart a new painting titled *Dancers at the Bar*. For years and years thereafter, whenever Degas came to visit his friend, he would look at *Dancers at the Bar* and say "That watering can is definitely idiotic, I simply must take it out!" Rouart thought the artist might be right, but having learned from experience, he never allowed Degas another try.

Later Years

When Degas was a young man he wrote, "If I can only find a good, simple, tranquil little wife who will understand my cranky humors and with whom I can spend a modest, hard-working life; isn't that a beautiful dream?" Over the years, the dream did not come true. Perhaps Degas was more truthful when he later said, "There is love, and there is work, we only have one heart." Degas choose to work very hard, and by the time he turned 60 years old he was famous. His paintings were bought for high prices by wealthy French and foreign collectors.

He should have been happy, but something terrible was happening to him. His eyesight, which troubled him most of his life, was failing. Degas was going blind. At the end of his painting career the colors he used grew brighter so that he could see what he was doing. As his eyesight worsened, his interest in sculpture increased. "Now that my sight is leaving me," he said, "I must take up a blind man's craft."

Sadly, during the last nine years of his life, he couldn't see well enough to paint or sculpt. Degas died at age 83. After his death, there was an avalanche of demand for Degas's work, and the prices of his paintings sharply rose.

Perhaps Degas is best described by the novelist Edmond de Goncourt, who said after meeting him, "An original fellow, this Degas. Among all the artists I have met so far, he is the one who has best been able, in representing modern life, to catch the spirit of that life."

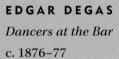

EDGAR DEGAS

Dancers at the Bar

c. 1876–77

Camera Capers

In 1888, an American named George Eastman introduced the first hand-held snapshot camera. He called it the Kodak (the word Kodak had no meaning but could be pronounced in all languages). Degas bought a portable Kodak and loved to carry it around with him. He used it to take pictures of his friends. He also used his camera to capture images that he could later refer to when painting a picture. Some of Degas's photos are so beautiful they can be considered works of art themselves.

Materials
Camera
Film
Money, to develop film
Painting supplies

1. Take your camera with you during the day to capture quick impressions. Try all of these techniques:

   • Stand above your subject and shoot down. This will work if someone is sitting on the floor or if you are shooting from a second-story window.

   • Stand below your subject and shoot up. Sit on the floor and aim at someone standing above you or stand at the bottom of the stairs or a hill and shoot this angle.

   • Crop your subject at the edge of the picture. To do this, begin by centering the subject in the viewfinder, then move the camera to the left or right before you snap the picture.

   • Take candid pictures. Capture someone who is not posing.

   • Take a blurry picture. Jiggle the camera as you snap a shot.

2. Once your film is developed, look for a photo that would make an interesting painting. Refer to it as you paint a picture.

What Degas Left Behind

In his lifetime, Degas's work was loved and his talents rewarded. After he died his friends and family entered his apartment and were amazed at what they discovered. The rooms were piled high with unsold paintings and early works he had bought back.

Many of these works are now in museums all over the world. Considered one of the finest artists of his time, Degas might actually be happy to know that his work now hangs in the most famous museums, next to the Old Masters that he loved.

Art Detective

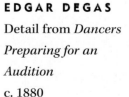

How to Spot a Degas
Here are some characteristics that will help you distinguish Degas's work:

- **Ballerinas!** Stretching, yawning, twirling, but never posing.
- **Racehorses!** Jockeys in colorful costumes.
- **Pastels!** Bright colors showing movement.
- **Unusual angles!** Look for slanted lines and bird's-eye views.

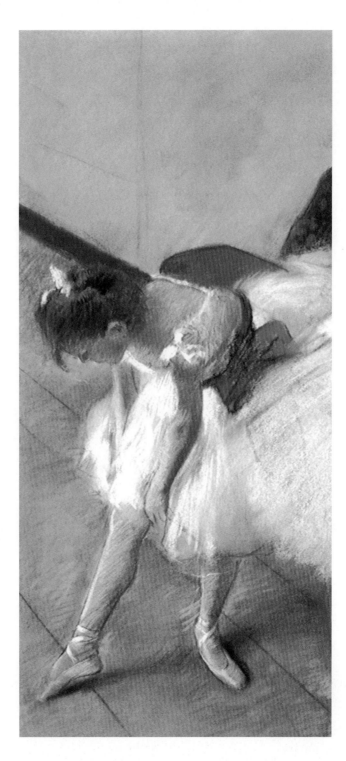

EDGAR DEGAS
Detail from *Dancers Preparing for an Audition*
c. 1880

MARY CASSATT

The Bath

1891–92

Mary Cassatt

Shortly after the First Impressionist Exhibition opened, Edgar Degas went to see what that year's Salon had to offer. Accompanied by his friend Joseph Tourny, he brusquely walked past painting after painting. As he suspected, very few paintings at the Salon impressed him. Suddenly Degas stopped in front of a portrait of a woman. Titled *Portrait of Madame Cortier*, it was a realistic portrayal of a middle-aged woman. It was carefully rendered, as an Old Master would have done, yet there was something very modern about it. After studying the painting for a few minutes, Degas turned to Tourny and announced, "Here is someone who feels as I do." The person who created this picture shared his ideas about how one should paint. The artist was an American named Mary Cassatt.

Degas couldn't believe the painting was the work of a woman. Not only was Mary Cassatt female, she wasn't even French! But he had to admit there was a similarity in their techniques. Their styles had the same carefully detailed, skillful drawing that made them different from most of the other Impressionists. It would be three years before Degas actually met Cassatt and a warm if sometimes rocky friendship would begin.

Mary Cassatt was born in Pennsylvania on May 22, 1844. America was still a baby itself. It had 26 states, and half of them still permitted slavery. It would be almost 80 years before women would be able to vote.

Cassatt grew up enjoying all the comforts of an upper-middle-class home. Servants handled the chores, and a nanny looked after Mary, her broth-

ers, and a sister. All this comfort came at a cost, however. Little girls from wealthy families didn't have much freedom. They had to act like little ladies, and they couldn't run around playing fun rough-and-tumble games like poor children could. Even so, Cassatt was very energetic. She had a quick temper, too.

Cassatt's father made his fortune in banking and real estate, but his favorite way to spend time was not working—he preferred to travel and spend time with his family. When Mary was seven years old, her father announced that the family would be moving to France. In the autumn of 1851, they set sail on one of the new steamships that were crossing the Atlantic. Cassatt spent most of this two-week trip seasick, but she quickly recovered when she saw Paris.

Little Mary thought Europe was wonderful; everything was so exotic. Her family's apartment was just off the Champs-Elysées, the city's most elegant street. She watched as exquisitely dressed men and women drove up and down the street in ornate horse-drawn coaches. The museums were fabulous! Some of them, like the Louvre, used to be royal palaces. Cassatt spent four exciting years in Europe. She even lived in Heidelberg, Germany, for a while. The Cassatts returned to America when Mary was 11 years old.

"I Want to Be an Artist"

By the time Cassatt was 16 she knew she wanted to be an artist. This presented a problem for her father, who thought studying art for a while was one thing, but in the 1800s no respectable woman in America would make a career of it. Respectable women should have no career at all! Girls were allowed to go to art school so they could polish up their parlor arts such as sketching, painting, embroidery, and piano playing. These skills mattered when trying to impress and attract a prospective young husband. Having a professional artist for a daughter didn't please Cassatt's father one bit. He said to her, "I would almost rather see you dead."

Once Mr. Cassatt recovered from his shock at her announcement, he suggested that she study at the Pennsylvania Academy of Fine Arts. He probably thought she'd eventually come to her senses. She agreed to the plan, even though it wasn't what she really wanted. She thought the only way to learn was by copying great works of art from the past. This was the way the artists in Europe learned, copying the masterpieces that hung in museums like the Louvre. The Pennsylvania Academy of Fine Arts was the oldest art school in America. Still, it didn't own any works by the Great Masters. America was too young to have great col-

MARY CASSATT
Lydia Leaning on Her Arms,
Seated in a Loge
c. 1879

lections of fine art hanging in its museums. One museum was very proud that at least it had a mastodon skeleton!

Cassatt knew that she had to study art in Europe. But how could she convince her father? Proper young women didn't travel to such faraway places. Luckily, the Cassatts still had friends living in France. She convinced her father that it would be good for her to visit old friends. And if she wanted to visit art museums in her spare time, all the better for her education. Her father agreed.

The year was 1861. Cassatt's plan to leave America couldn't have come at a worse time. Abraham Lincoln recently had been elected president and the Civil War had just begun. It was impossible for her to leave the country until the war ended. She put her plans on hold for four years.

Life in Paris

Cassatt was 22 when she finally arrived in Paris. Her clothes were expensive and fashionable; her mother had seen to that. Of course she was properly chaperoned wherever she went; her father had seen to that.

Her first discovery was a disappointment. She soon found out that France's most prestigious art school, the École des Beaux-Arts, didn't admit female students. She tried taking private art lessons, but she quickly became dissatisfied with all

her instructors. She thought the paintings at the Louvre were her best teachers. Most days she could be found there, seated on a high stool, wearing a smock over her street clothes. Cassatt would set her easel alongside dozens of other aspiring artists who came to copy the Masters. Her chaperone, usually an older friend or her sister, stayed nearby. It was only two years before the Paris art world recognized Cassatt's talent. The Salon accepted her painting of a young woman playing a mandolin. It was 1868. Her career was taking off.

Becoming an Impressionist

Cassatt's excitement about the Salon faded over the next seven years. In 1875, she submitted a portrait of her sister Lydia to the Salon. Back it came: rejected. She was told the colors were too bright. She put it back on her easel and painted the background darker. The following year the judges accepted it. They were pleased that it no longer had such garish colors, like those used by the lunatic Impressionists. But Cassatt thought the painting was no longer as good.

Just when Cassatt began to doubt the decisions of the Salon, a visitor came to her studio—a dark, slender, well-dressed man with passionate opinions about art. His name was Edgar Degas—one of the lunatics. At 43 he was 10 years older than Cassatt; he was also a better known and more accomplished artist, and she knew his art well. In fact, his work confirmed her own ideas about using bold colors and unblended brush strokes. She felt honored to receive Degas at her studio. When he asked her to give up the Salon and exhibit with his friends the Impressionists, she "accepted with joy." "Already I had recognized those who were my true masters," she said. "I began to live."

Cassatt's debut with the Impressionists was a great success, at least for her. It was the fourth exhibit of the group, and the critics were still outraged by the "infantile daubing" of Monet and Renoir. The work of Degas and Cassatt, however, showed "unusual distinction in rendering," according to one critic. He appreciated that their subjects were carefully drawn. By now, even Cassatt's father could see that Mary was on the threshold of a promising career. Both of her parents expressed pride in her success and sent newspaper clippings of her reviews to other family members. Cassatt felt proud to be one of the Impressionists. She used her profits from the show to buy two paintings, one by Monet and one by Degas.

Cassatt's Methods

Mary Cassatt painted what she knew best—life at home. In the 1800s, it wasn't thought to be proper for well-brought-up women to be seen by themselves at cafés, train stations, or even on city

BERTHE MORISOT

Mary Cassatt wasn't the only female Impressionist to make a name for herself. Another member of the group was French artist Berthe Morisot. Like Cassatt, she too came from a wealthy family and could only venture out where "respectable ladies" were allowed. As a result, Morisot also painted domestic scenes of life in an upper-class home.

Morisot's love for art began when she was 16 years old. Her mother decided to give her father a surprise by having his daughters produce pictures for his birthday. This required that the three girls take painting lessons. After the birthday surprise, Berthe and her sister Edma wanted to continue their lessons. Knowing how talented the girls were, their teacher tried to warn their mother. "My teaching will not endow them with minor drawing room accomplishments; they will become painters. Do you realize what this means?" he asked. "This will be revolutionary, I might say catastrophic."

Both sisters did become accomplished artists, and their work was accepted by the Salon. Edma gave up painting once she married, as was considered proper for that time. Berthe, however, did not stop painting even after she was married. She pursued her career and joined the Impressionists. At the First Impressionist Exhibition, her painting *The Cradle* (see page 11) was one of the few successes. The subject of the painting—a mother lovingly looking down at her baby—touched the visitors.

Morisot was very good friends with Édouard Manet. He painted portraits of her. They first met at the Louvre, where she was copying a painting by Rubens. In 1874, the same year as the First Impressionist Exhibition, Morisot got married. Her groom was Manet's younger brother, Eugène.

Every Picture Tells a Story

Mary Cassatt's pictures bring us into someone's house, usually, without being noticed. We see little slices of life that tell us a story. This game gives you the fun of making up a story and is a good memory exercise. Try this game with Cassatt's painting, Young Mother Sewing. *You'll discover that in this picture, someone does notice that we are watching.*

Materials

10 index cards
Pencil or pen
Your imagination
2 or more players

1. Write one phrase on each index card that begins a statement about the scene in a picture. Here are some suggestions:

   The name(s) of the person (people) in this picture is (are) _____ .

   They just finished _____ .
   They are thinking about _____ .

   Next they will _____ .
   What we can't see in this picture is _____ .

   It's too bad that _____ .
   The good news is _____ .
   Soon they will leave to go to _____ .

   Next year they will _____ .
   They are feeling _____ because _____ .
   If only they knew _____ .

2. To play bring out a picture for the game. This can be a painting, a photograph, or a picture in a book. Place the index cards face down and shuffle them. The first player chooses a card and reads the card's statement out loud. She fills in the blank in the statement by making up a story based on the action in the picture. The next player chooses a card, repeats the story already told about the picture, and then reads the statement on this card and adds on to the story. Take turns adding to the story until all the cards are used.

   Note: If there are no people in the picture, use statements such as:
   This place is called _____ .

MARY CASSATT

Young Mother Sewing

c. 1900

streets. Young ladies enjoyed dressing up in their finest gowns, draped in jewels, to attend the opera. But they wouldn't dream of going backstage to watch the performers rehearse. Because Cassatt was a respectable woman, she simply could not paint the same subjects as her male Impressionist friends such as Degas.

More than anything Cassatt loved to paint images of children, often with their mothers. The people in her paintings do not seem to be posing for their portraits. It's as if we are peeking at them through a keyhole. They don't know we're watching them as they listen to a story being read or snuggle together in a hug. Traditionally, artists didn't paint pictures of unposed, relaxed subjects. Even when posing for a photographic portrait, children and adults were held still by hidden head clamps. Otherwise, the photo might be blurry. Unposed, Cassatt's paintings capture the moment in a quick impression.

One thing Cassatt didn't do was make people look better than they did in real life. An ungrateful relative once returned a portrait to her. The nose was too big! Painting children was a much better option. They might wiggle and squirm when she drew them, but at least they didn't complain about the size of their noses.

Whatever her subject, Cassatt's pictures are bright and colorful. Like her friend Degas, Cassatt carefully rendered her image. She used pastels, too.

A Japanese Influence

One spring day in 1890, when she was 46 years old, Cassatt saw an art exhibit that inspired her to try something new. A major exhibition of Japanese woodblock prints was held at the École des Beaux-Arts. Degas had often talked to Cassatt about how talented Japanese artists were. Still, she was not enthusiastic until she saw the exhibit.

At the time, Japan seemed remote and mysterious. The people in France were just beginning to learn about its art. Now 725 prints were on display in Paris. Degas knew the exhibit would be incredible and took Cassatt to see the work. The prints impressed her so much that she returned to study them again and again. Then she set out to make her own. Over the next year she made a series of 10 color prints. Cassatt used her own subject matter, but her lines and colors show a Japanese influence. In her print *The Letter*, she used flat areas of color, patterns of scattered flowers, and a simple design—just like the prints from Japan. She even gave the woman in her print Asian facial features.

How Cassatt Made Her Etchings

Making an etched print was a long, difficult process. First, Cassatt made a picture by scratching lines and shapes onto a copper plate. Next, she sprinkled powdered rosin onto parts of the plate where she wanted texture in her picture. For this purpose, she had to heat the plate and soak it in acid. She made a separate plate for each color.

To make a print, Cassatt rubbed ink onto the first plate, then wiped it off with a rag. This left only the etched lines, shapes, and textures inked. She called the little twisted rags she used *poupees*, which means "rag dolls."

After all that, Cassatt was ready to print her picture. She dampened a sheet of paper, placed it on the plate, and ran them both through an etching press. When the machine pressed them together, the dampness of the paper drew the remaining ink out of the plate and onto the paper. She had to do this for each color, using the same piece of paper. She needed to carefully line up each plate so that the color printed in exactly the right area.

MARY CASSATT
The Letter
1890–91

Recognition from Home

Although Cassatt was becoming well known in France, it disappointed her that people in her own country didn't know her work. In 1892 she received a visitor named Mrs. Bertha Palmer, a prominent figure in Chicago society. Palmer was in charge of the Women's Pavilion of the World's Columbian Exhibition (better know as the Chicago World's Fair) scheduled to be held in 1893. She asked Cassatt to paint a huge mural depicting modern women for the exhibition. Cassatt was thrilled. Now thousands of Americans would be able to see her artwork.

It was not an easy job. Cassatt had never painted anything so large: the mural was to be 12 by 58 feet (3.6 by 17.4 meters). She had a special studio built for the three huge canvases. She divided her mural into three parts: the middle panel showed *Young Women Plucking the Fruits of Knowledge and Science*, while the two side panels showed *Young Girls Pursuing Fame* and *Arts, Music, Dancing*.

Unfortunately, the mural was hung so high up in the huge building that it was hard to see. After the fair, the Women's Pavilion was dismantled. No one knows what happened to Cassatt's mural. It was probably destroyed. Her dream of becoming well known in America was not to happen yet.

Cassatt would have to wait six more years for America to discover her work. In 1899 a New York exhibit of her work received recognition. Finally, Cassatt was becoming known in her own country.

Working for Women's Rights

Cassatt didn't travel back to America often. The only way to get there from Europe was by ship, and Cassatt never outgrew her seasickness. During a visit in 1908, she became interested in a movement that was stirring up trouble in America. The movement was for women's right to vote, also known as the Women's Suffrage Movement. Like everything she did, Cassatt jumped in full force. All her life she had to fight for the right to be respected as a professional artist. Now she was ready to fight for the rights of all women. She actively recruited other women to join the movement, too. "I do hope you are going to be interested in the suffrage," she wrote to one young artist.

In 1915 Cassatt sent five works to a New York City exhibition to benefit the suffrage movement. Unfortunately, most people stayed away from the exhibit because they didn't agree with the idea of letting women vote. It took five more years for the suffragists to gain American women the right to vote.

Chateau de Beaufresne

When Cassatt was 50 years old, she purchased a beautiful château in the French countryside, very near Monet's home, Giverny. Over the years, her home filled with family members. Her parents and sister lived with her for many years. The house often rang with the laughter of visiting nieces and nephews.

Cassatt never married and had no children. But she had a lot of pets. Little dogs that she raised scampered all through the house. She also had a parrot named Coco. Degas once wrote a poem in honor of this boisterous member of Cassatt's family. Some people wondered if Cassatt and Degas had ever planned to get married—they were such good friends. It remains a secret, because she burned all his letters before she died.

Cassatt lived a long life of 82 years. Sadly, she had to stop painting at age 70 because she was going blind.

In her lifetime, Cassatt achieved what many artists never experience—recognition. In 1904, the French government presented her with the distinguished Legion of Honor medal. This award was rarely given to a woman, much less an American.

Bringing Art to America

During her lifetime Mary Cassatt did much more than just create great works of art. She was responsible for bringing to America many of the Impressionist paintings that we see in U.S. museums today.

One hundred years ago Cassatt convinced many of her wealthy friends to buy the latest style of art coming out of France. She guided two of her friends, Mr. and Mrs. Havemeyer, as they acquired one of the finest art collections in America. Their acquisitions included some of the best works by Monet, Degas, Renoir, and Manet. This also helped out her fellow artists, who were often desperate for the money American sales could bring. Louise Havemeyer (at the time, Louise Elder) trusted Cassatt's advice and bought her first Degas pastel

Art Detective

How to Spot a Cassatt
Here are some characteristics that will help you distinguish Cassatt's work:

➤ **Mother and child!** Simply passing a quiet moment together.
➤ **Home Sweet Home!** Slices of family life, unposed and relaxed.
➤ **Girl with red hair!** That's Mary's sister, Lydia—one of her favorite models.
➤ **Pastels!**

when she was still a schoolgirl. (Remember this from the previous chapter?)

Not only did Cassatt concern herself with placing modern works of art in American collections; she also encouraged buyers to acquire paintings by such great European masters as Titian, Velazquez, and Rembrandt. In this way she hoped to bring more fine art to her native country so that young American art students would have more opportunities to study great art at home.

What Cassatt Has Given Us

By the time Mary Cassatt died she had achieved every goal she set out to accomplish. She could proudly look at the great collections of European art in America and know she played a role in bringing them here. As she predicted, these pieces eventually made their way from private collections into American art museums. When Louise Havemeyer died, she left most of her extensive collection to the Metropolitan Museum of Art in New York.

During her lifetime, Cassatt was also able to see another dream come true—her work became as well loved in America as it was in France. Today, her heartwarming scenes of mothers and children adorn museum walls, waiting patiently for us to enjoy them.

MARY CASSATT

The Cup of Tea

1879

Like the Impressionists, the Post-Impressionists didn't choose their name. In fact, most of them never heard the name at all. The term was invented for an exhibit of their work many years after most of them had died.

Three of the artists, Paul Cézanne, Paul Gauguin, and Georges Seurat, showed their work at the Impressionist Exhibitions. Like the Impressionists, they chose bright colors, but they tried new ways of using them. Each in his own way took what was learned from the Impressionists and went a step further.

PAUL GAUGUIN
Matamoe (Landscape with Peacocks)
1892

PAUL CÉZANNE

Still Life with Curtain and
Flowered Pitcher

c. 1898–99

Paul Cézanne

In 1894, when Mary Cassatt lived in her chateau near Giverny, she was invited to the home of her neighbor, Claude Monet. Another guest was invited, too. She had never met him in person, but she owned one of his paintings. When she finally did meet him, it was memorable. "When I first saw him," Cassatt wrote to a friend, "he looked like a cut-throat with large red eyeballs standing out from his head in a most ferocious manner, a rather fierce-looking pointed beard, quite grey, and an excited way of talking that positively made the dishes rattle . . . in spite of the total disregard for the dictionary of manners, he shows a politeness towards us which no other man would have shown." This man was the artist Paul Cézanne.

Later, Monet gave a small dinner party in Cézanne's honor. Guests included Pierre Auguste Renoir, Mary Cassatt, and Alfred Sisley, another Impressionist. As they sat down to eat, Monet told Cézanne how fond they were of him, and how much they admired his work. Cézanne's eyes filled with tears. "Ah, Monet, even you make fun of me," he said as he rose and left the room before anyone could stop him. He left Giverny immediately. He didn't even take time to gather the paintings he was working on.

At age 55, this sensitive, shy, and often gruff artist was still struggling to make a name for himself, but one day he would be called the father of Modern Art.

APPLES

many of Cézanne's still lifes have apples in them. Some people think he painted apples as a symbol of his friendship with Zola. He never forgot the basket of apples that sealed their friendship. Cézanne once said with a wink, "You know, Cézanne's apples have their origins in a very distant past!"

PAUL CÉZANNE
Detail from *Still Life with Curtain and Flowered Pitcher* c. 1898–99

A Shy Country Boy

Paul Cézanne was born in Aix-en-Provence on January 19, 1839. Aix (pronounced EX) is in a beautiful, sunny region of southern France. Cézanne's father owned the local bank and was very wealthy. Even though young Cézanne grew up in a mansion with many servants, his boyhood wasn't very happy. His father was very strict with Paul and his two younger sisters. His mother, who came from a poor family and never learned to read or write, loved her children very much and tried to make up for their father's domineering ways.

When Cézanne was 13 years old, his father sent him to live at a boarding school. Cézanne excelled in his classes but was very shy and didn't have many friends. One day he noticed a group of students teasing a skinny boy with glasses. It took a lot of courage, but Cézanne defended him against the bullies. The next day the boy brought Cézanne a basket of apples as a way of saying thank you. His name was Émile Zola. One day Zola would become a famous writer.

Zola and Cézanne became best friends. They loved to hike in the beautiful countryside of Provence, a hilly landscape that would one day be Cézanne's favorite subject to paint. While they hiked, they made up poems. Cézanne had talent with words. "Poetically you are more gifted than I am," Zola once told him. "You write with your heart." Cézanne did very well in most of his studies. He won prizes in his math, Latin, and Greek classes but was never able to draw attention to himself in his art lessons. Surprisingly, Zola received better grades for drawing than Cézanne. Still, Cézanne enjoyed sketching and painting, and after taking extra lessons at the local art academy, he won second place in a competition.

Even though the friends had first met because Cézanne defended Zola, when they were older it was Zola who became Cézanne's greatest supporter. Zola had more power to assert himself and knew how to rouse his sensitive friend, who often felt unsure of himself. When Zola completed his classes, he left for Paris to pursue a career as a writer. Cézanne thought he'd like to join him there and go to art school. But his father had a different plan.

Artist or Lawyer?

Cézanne's father was a very practical businessman and thought his son must be mad to want to do such a silly thing as study art. He had other plans for his son. His father needed someone who could run the bank when he retired, and he had already decided that law school was his son's next step. It was obvious to Cézanne that a career as a lawyer was not what he wanted. Defeated, he agreed to his father's wishes. "Alas, I have taken the crooked path of the law," Cézanne wrote to Zola. "'Taken' is not the word—I have been forced to take it!"

Cézanne studied at law school, but he hated it. Meanwhile, he continued his art education by taking drawing and painting lessons during his free time. He spent as little time as possible on his legal studies, and occasionally he missed a lecture in order to visit an art museum. After two years, his father had to admit that Cézanne was not cut out to be a lawyer. Unexpectedly, he gave in and agreed to support his son with a small allowance while he studied art in Paris.

Unfortunately, moving to Paris didn't make Cézanne any happier. He was 22 years old, and it was the first time he had been away from Provence. He felt like an outsider, not comfortable with the sophisticated ways of the city dwellers. The shy country boy was terribly homesick. To make matters worse, Cézanne concealed his shyness by acting gruff and unfriendly.

Cézanne tried taking lessons at a private art studio but was so sensitive to criticism he became a class joke. When he was upset, he would either fly into a rage or stomp off and disappear for days. He also realized that the other students were more advanced than he was. They'd been studying art longer and had more technical skills. After five stressful months, he packed his bags and returned to Aix.

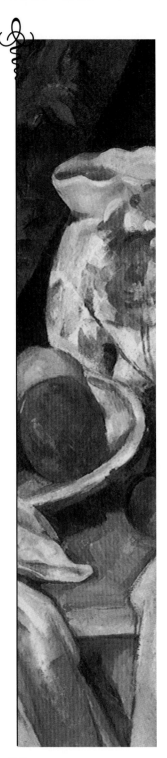

Back home, Cézanne worked as a clerk at his father's bank. But he never gave up his dream of becoming an artist. He'd doodle in the bank's ledger books, writing poems such as:

"My father the banker does not see without fear
Behind his desk a painter appear."

Sometimes he didn't bother going to work at all. He preferred to wander the countryside gazing at the landscape. That summer, Zola came back to visit Provence and convinced Cézanne to return to Paris with him and try again.

His second visit to Paris was much more successful. At age 23 his life as a painter was about to begin. Cézanne began meeting with other young artists, such as Monet and Renoir, at the Café Guerbois. But he was still his old moody self.

It didn't seem like a friendly social gathering to Cézanne. The other artists who met at the café thought he dressed like a peasant, in shabby, dirty clothes. Meanwhile, Manet appeared elegant in his top hat and carefully trimmed beard—like the rich gentleman he was. And Monet wore starched shirts with lace cuffs—pretending to be a rich gentleman. It all annoyed Cézanne. When he went to the café, he would sit apart from the group. Silent and frowning, he appeared lost in his thoughts. But if anyone said something he disagreed with, he could lose his temper and argue ferociously. Or he could just as easily abruptly get up and walk out without saying good-bye. It didn't win him many friends.

He did have one friend among the artists, though. His name was Camille Pissarro, one of the older artists. He was patient with Cézanne's prickly moods and treated him like a son. They often put their easels side by side and painted landscapes together. Pissarro encouraged Cézanne and helped him with his painting.

Camille Pissarro

Camille Pissarro could be described as the father of the Impressionist movement. Born in 1830, he was the oldest Impressionist and the only one to show in every Impressionist Exhibition. He was the most open and understanding of his group and the younger painters turned to him for advice and art lessons. Pissarro wasn't an innovator. He tried many painting techniques during his painting career including Impressionism and pointillism. Today, his paintings of serene countrysides, which were his specialty, are prized. Unfortunately, this wasn't the case during his lifetime. True success eluded him. "I remain at the tail end of Impressionism," he once noted sadly.

Cézanne's Methods

Things that stood still! That's what Cézanne liked to paint. A big, solid mountain or a well-behaved basket of fruit was much easier to deal with than a

A FRIENDSHIP ENDS

Émile Zola became a famous novelist. He also wrote articles that supported the new art called Impressionism. But in 1886, when the Impressionist artists were still struggling, Zola wrote a novel titled *L'Oeuvre* ("The Masterpiece"). In it he tells the story of an artist named Claude Lantier. Lantier dreams of greatness but finds only failure and eventually commits suicide. Because Zola described his character using information he knew about his artist friends' lives, his fictional story seemed too real for some. Several of these artists thought the fictional Lantier was based upon themselves. "Have you read Zola's book?" Monet wrote to fellow artist Pissarro, "I am afraid it will do us a lot of harm." Cézanne felt so sure that Zola was writing about him that he ended their 34-year friendship. Cézanne never talked to Zola again.

squirming model. When he did paint pictures of people, he often made them pose as many as 100 times for one painting. "Be still like an apple!" he once scolded a model.

Cézanne's paintings seem to be made up of many rectangular patches of color. His goal, he said, was "to make something solid and durable out of Impressionism." In fact, he wasn't an Impressionist at all. His brush strokes are dense and solid, like colorful toy building blocks. They're very different from Monet's loose dabs of shimmering color or Renoir's feathery, comma-shaped strokes. Cézanne also thought that shapes found in nature, like trees and mountains, should be simplified. "Interpret nature in terms of the cylinder, the sphere, the cone," he wrote. Because of all his new ideas, Cézanne is called a Post-Impressionist.

Unlike Monet, who worked fast to capture the light, Cézanne worked very slowly. It took him so long to paint a basket of fruit that it usually began to rot before he was finished. Cézanne solved that problem by using artificial fruit as his models.

When it came to painting, Cézanne was an expert at breaking the rules.

Rule 1: Things should appear smaller in the background than in the foreground. This is called linear perspective. Cézanne thought that if something was important in his painting, it shouldn't shrink just because it was in the distance. If he painted a landscape with a moun-

Still Life à la Cézanne

Roll out the fruit! It's time to make a still life. Try the same coloring tricks Cézanne used in Still Life with Three Peaches *to see how he showed perspective.*

Materials

2 pieces of paper   3 pieces of fruit, any variety
Pencil   Crayons, markers, or colored pencils

1. Using a pencil, draw a line from left to right across one piece of paper. The area below the line will be the tabletop.

2. On the tabletop, draw the outlines of 3 pieces of fruit: a pear, an orange, and a lemon (or whatever fruit you have). Overlap the fruit to show that some pieces are in front of others.

3. Repeat steps 1 and 2 on the second piece of paper. (Hint: You can trace the picture by holding the papers up to a sunlit window.)

4. Color the fruit in one of the pictures using warm colors, such as yellow, orange, and red. Color the background using cool colors, such as blue and lavender. Color the wooden tabletop brown. Set this picture aside.

5. On the second sheet of paper, reverse where the warm and cool colors are placed. Think of these pieces of fruit as a dark green pear, a plum, and a lime. Color them using cool colors like purple, olive green, and dark green. Color the background using warm colors such as red and yellow. Color the wooden tabletop brown.

6. Compare the two pictures to see which is more effective in showing perspective. (The yellow and orange fruit should stand out from the background more effectively because warm colors advance while cool colors recede.)

Here's a coloring tip: If you look at a real piece of fruit, you'll see many colors on it. A yellow pear, for example, is made up of many shades of yellow. It may also have a bit of green or orange on parts of it. When you paint your fruit, use more than one color.

PAUL CÉZANNE

Still Life with Three Peaches
1885–87

PEAS FOR PAINTINGS

Cézanne traded his paintings for food to feed his family after his father drastically cut his allowance. The local grocer was told that it would be a wise investment to barter with this soon-to-be-famous artist. Cézanne also exchanged artwork for tubes of paint from Julien Tanguy, an art supplier in Paris. Many struggling artists traded their canvases with Tanguy, including Vincent van Gogh. Before his death in 1893, Tanguy was considered Cézanne's art dealer and his store was the only place to see Cézanne's work. Young artists who had heard about Cézanne flocked to Tanguy's shop to look at Cézanne's work as if they were going to a museum.

tain, he made the mountain big, even if in a photograph it would appear as a little speck. Mountains are important, he thought, and they should be big.

Rule 2: Colors are lighter and objects are fuzzy if they're in the distance. This is called aerial perspective. Cézanne thought every part of the picture was equally important. He painted distant objects with bold, clear colors, just like the objects in the front of his picture.

PAUL CÉZANNE
View of Gardanne
1885–86

So how did he show perspective? Cézanne had other tricks up his sleeve. One simple way he showed depth was by overlapping objects. If he wanted to show that an orange was toward the front of a plate of fruit, and an apple was toward the back, he would paint the entire orange shape, overlapping, or blocking off, part of the apple shape.

Cézanne also used color to show depth. He knew that areas painted with blues and greens seem to recede or appear farther away in a picture. On the other hand, areas colored orange, red, or yellow seem to jump forward to the front of a picture. When Cézanne painted a still life, he colored his fruit yellow and orange and his backgrounds blue or green. *Voilà!* Cézanne's paintings show perspective.

The Lone Artist

Even though Cézanne had a few friends, he preferred to paint on his own. He often left Paris to spend time at home in Provence, where his father allowed him to convert part of their mansion into a studio.

Cézanne was often seen roaming the countryside of Provence with his painting equipment strapped to his back. His favorite subject was a nearby mountain, Mont Sainte-Victoire. Sometimes Monet and Renoir traveled to Provence and joined him on these outings. They admired Cézanne's skill, so they learned to tolerate his personality. Cézanne was intense about his art—even when painting *en plein air*, overlooking the peaceful countryside. When things didn't go right, he'd rip a painting from his easel, throw it to the ground, and leave it there. One day, as Renoir was hiking alone in these hills, he stumbled upon a "magnificent watercolor by Cézanne." Cézanne, apparently, did not agree with this opinion.

When Cézanne was 30 years old, he fell in love with a 19-year-old artists' model named Hortense Fiquet. She was tall and lovely, with long brown hair and big dark eyes. Hortense modeled for Cézanne, and he eventually convinced her to move in with him. Secretly, he set up household in a town not far from his parents' home in Aix. He continued to spend time with his parents as well as with Hortense. Cézanne kept Hortense secret because he was afraid his father wouldn't approve and therefore would stop giving him an allowance. Cézanne felt his father would never accept a union between his son and a girl who didn't have a dowry. (It was common in the 1800s for girls from wealthy families to have dowries—valuables such as money or property that was included in the marriage contract.) Perhaps Cézanne's father was suspicious that Hortense, who came from a lower class, would only be interested in the Cézanne fortune.

Three years later Hortense and Cézanne had a son and named him Paul. Cézanne loved his little boy, but he kept Paul a secret from his father as well. He dreaded being found out. When Paul was six years old, in 1878, Cézanne's father did find out. He was in the habit of opening Cézanne's mail, and in one letter a friend referred to "Madame Cézanne" and "Little Paul." Cézanne denied it all when asked. His infuriated father cut his allowance in half. Since his artwork seldom sold, Cézanne now had very little money to support his family.

A Change of Heart

In 1886, when Cézanne's father was 88 years old, he reluctantly agreed to the marriage of his son to Hortense. Cézanne's sister Marie was behind the reconciliation. She knew that Cézanne had an illegitimate son (who was now 14), and, because she was a devoted Catholic, she thought marriage would save Cézanne from a sinful life. Ironically, after being together for 17 years, the newlyweds had already grown apart. Hortense spent most of her time in Paris with their son while Cézanne remained in Provence. His father died a few months after their reconciliation. Cézanne inherited his family's wealth. His financial troubles were finally over.

AMBROISE VOLLARD

Ambroise Vollard was a young art dealer in Paris when Pissarro introduced him to his friend Cézanne. Vollard was new to the business and lacked confidence in his own taste, but he had the sense to listen to Pissarro's advice. Pissarro encouraged Vollard to get in touch with the 56-year-old Cézanne. As a result, Cézanne sent him 150 pictures and Vollard arranged an exhibition at his gallery. (By this time, the Salon was losing its hold as the only place in town to see great art.) Not all the critics appreciated Cézanne's work. One, however, was thrilled. "Passers-by walking into the Galerie Vollard will be faced with about 50 pictures, from which they can finally reach a verdict on one of the finest and greatest personalities of our time. . . . He will end up in the Louvre," wrote Gustave Geffroy.

Exhibiting with the Impressionists

For many years, Cézanne submitted his paintings to the Salon, but the answer was always the same: rejected. When he exhibited at the First Impressionist Exhibition in 1874, he received dismal reviews. He stirred up more excitement in 1877, when he decided to try again at the Third Impressionist Exhibition. As always, the critics showed up. Louis Leroy, the critic who had first named the Impressionists, had something to say about one of Cézanne's portraits. Cézanne had painted the portrait using new color ideas. The man's face is a yellowish hue, touched with red. His hair is blue, highlighted in gray-green. In his review, Leroy warned pregnant women that viewing the picture would infect their unborn child with yellow fever. Critics thought it was obvious that this portrait of Cézanne's friend, Victor Chocquet, didn't look anything like Victor. Any person who came to the exhibit could plainly see this, since Victor himself was on hand every single day to defend the portrait and praise its creator. But nobody else shared Victor's enthusiasm. After the dismal reviews, Cézanne never exhibited with the Impressionists again.

An Undiscovered Talent

For most of Cézanne's life, only the small circle of artists who knew him recognized his talent. Fortunately, before his father died in 1886, he had a change of heart. He left his son a large inheritance. Cézanne became financially independent. He could have enjoyed his fortune living in comfort and traveling the world, but instead Cézanne continued to live a quiet, simple life in Provence. Hortense preferred living in Paris, which also suited Cézanne.

When Cézanne was in his early sixties, he began a series of large paintings of bathers sunning themselves on the bank of a stream. It's a classical motif, something artists had been painting for hundreds of years. But Cézanne's renditions look very modern. This is because he used the same technique of applying solid patches of contrasting colors as he did in his landscapes and still lifes. Each painting took years to complete. For his models, he referred to sketches and reproductions of paintings from the Louvre and elsewhere. And he relied on his memory. "Painting is in here," he said, tapping his head.

Toward the end of his life, Cézanne could be seen in Aix, walking to the edge of town, carrying

PAUL CÉZANNE

Houses in Provence (Vicinity of L'Estaque)

1879–82

his box of watercolors. From here he could look across the fields and woods to his favorite model, Mont Sainte-Victoire.

That was where he was one October day in 1906, when he got caught in a sudden rainstorm. Walking home, he became chilled and weakened, and he collapsed in the road. A passerby found him unconscious and took him home. Seven days later he died from pneumonia. His wife and son were notified but arrived too late. Cézanne was 67.

The Father of Modern Art

After his death, Cézanne's reputation grew with astounding speed as several exhibitions honored him. An exhibit featuring 56 of Cézanne's paintings was held at the Paris Autumn Salon, where it won considerable acclaim. Many young artists visited this exhibition, including Pablo Picasso and Henri Matisse. These artists saw how Cézanne reduced nature into simple geometric shapes and how he used bold colors. He's been given credit for paving the way for the next generation of artists, such as the Cubists and Fauves. Today, Cézanne is called the father of Modern Art.

ART DETECTIVE

How to Spot a Cézanne
Here are some characteristics that help distinguish Cézanne's work:

- **Still lifes!** Yellow apples and orange peaches on a tabletop. Look for blue-green walls.
- **Landscapes!** Intense colors applied in rectangular patches—especially mountains.
- **Tipsy tabletops!** Fruit looks like it could roll off the table and into your hand.
- **Solid, dense colors!** And, perhaps, not at all true to nature—such as blue faces.

Activity

Stenciling Cézanne

If you look at Cézanne's painting Houses in Provence, *you'll notice that it's made up of many colorful rectangles. Cézanne is famous for this painting technique. Try it out for yourself, using a potato instead of a paintbrush! Adult help suggested.*

Materials

Potato	Tempera or acrylic paints—
Knife	blue, green, and yellow
Cutting board	Water
Paper	Shallow plates for paint
Pencil	Surface for stencil, such as
Leaf from a tree	paper or paper bag
Scissors	

1. Cut a potato into small rectangles, about 1 x 1½ inches (2.5 x 3 cm).

2. Trace the shape of the leaf on a piece of paper. Carefully puncture a hole along the edge of the leaf and cut out the inside of the shape to make a stencil.

3. Look carefully at Cézanne's painting *Houses in Provence*. Notice how he colored the painting using only blues, greens, and yellows. Use these colors to stencil a leaf design. Pour a small amount of paint, mixed with a few drops of water, onto a plate, one for each color. Place the stencil over the area you wish to paint. Dip a piece of potato into one color and press it inside the stencil area. Continue stamping, overlapping the rectangles a bit, filling in the design.

Another Impression: Use red, orange, and yellow to stencil an autumn leaf. Stencil your own wrapping paper, or make colorful stationery.

PAUL GAUGUIN

Nave Nave Moe
(Delightful Drowsiness)
1894

Paul Gauguin

The Fifth Impressionist Exhibition was held in 1880, a year that began with a cold icy winter. The artists who loved to paint outdoors stayed bundled up inside their studios. It was a gloomy beginning to an unhappy year for the group.

The following spring, when the exhibition opened, Monet and Renoir refused to be part of it. They were furious that a new artist whose work they didn't like would be allowed to enter his paintings. This artist wasn't a serious painter, they argued. He was a wealthy stockbroker who only dabbled on Sundays. He lived in a big warm house and played at painting, while they were in their cold studios with hardly enough coal to cook their beans.

Monet and Renoir thought their small group of very talented artists shouldn't welcome amateurs. "The small church," declared Monet, "has become a banal school which opens its doors to the first dauber who knocks." Other artists in the group, such as Edgar Degas, didn't agree. He thought the new artist had talent. So, in April 1880, the exhibition opened without the paintings of the two most famous, though poor, Impressionists, Monet and Renoir. That year, their work would hang on the walls of a building down the street. They were in the Salon! The artist who created such a stir was Paul Gauguin.

How did Monet get the Salon to accept his work? (At this point in his life, he was desperate to earn some money.) It's best explained in a letter he wrote to a friend: "For the Salon, I had to do something more restrained and bourgeois." *Bourgeois* (boor-JWA) is a French word that means "middle class." It also implies an unimaginative attitude, overly concerned with luxuries.

An Exciting Beginning

Paul Gauguin was born in Paris on June 7, 1848. Outside, on the streets of Paris, a battle was raging. The citizens of Paris were rising up because there were no jobs and the people were starving. Later that year, Louis-Napoléon Bonaparte was elected president. (When he was unable to run for a second term he forcefully made himself Emperor Napoléon III.)

Whether Louis-Napoléon was elected was very important to the Gauguin family. Gauguin's father, a political journalist for a French newspaper, wrote articles that didn't support the new president. He thought France would be much better off without Louis-Napoléon. This was a risky stand to take. Criticizing the government could get a person

thrown in prison. This was what Gauguin's father was thinking one year later when he decided to move his family to South America.

Growing Up in Peru

Gauguin was only one year old when his family boarded a ship for South America. They were headed for Lima, Peru, where his mother's wealthy relative named Pio lived. Gauguin's father hoped Uncle Pio would help him start a newspaper of his own in Lima. Sadly, Gauguin's father died during the long journey across the ocean. Instead of arriving in Lima filled with excitement for a bright future, Gauguin's mother arrived as a poor widow, alone in a strange land with two small children. Luckily, Uncle Pio, who was said to be over 100 years old, was thrilled to add the three newcomers to his large family. His house was one of the biggest in Lima, and there was room for everyone. For Gauguin, it seemed like an exotic fairy tale. He was able to meet people he would never have known in France—Chinese, Native Americans, and Africans were a part of his daily life. Peru was very different from France—children had monkeys for pets. People in Lima didn't worry about thunderstorms because it hardly ever rained, and they got used to waking up in a shaking bed because of the frequent earthquakes.

A WRITER IN EXILE

It was common for writers who spoke against the government to be punished for their thoughts. Victor Hugo, a famous poet and novelist, was also a committed political activist. In his popular books, including *The Hunchback of Notre Dame*, he spoke out against the social injustices he saw in France, such as poverty and homelessness. He also spoke out for freedom of the press, the right to a free education, and other ideas that the new emperor opposed. Napoléon III saw Hugo's writings as a criticism of his government. It's not safe to criticize a dictator. To escape prison camp, Hugo left France and went into exile, which lasted 19 years. During that time Hugo wrote one of his most famous books, *Les Miserables*. Hugo became a symbol of freedom to French people during his exile, and after the 1870 overthrow of Napoléon III, he returned to France in triumph. When Hugo died, 500,000 people lined the streets of Paris to mourn him.

Gauguin lived in South America for five exciting years. Everything he saw there looked big and bright—vividly patterned butterflies, brilliantly colored fruits, and masses of fragrant flowers. France seemed very far away to this little boy who had only learned to speak Spanish.

Gauguin was seven years old when the fairy tale come to an end. His mother thought it was time for him to go to school in his native country, so the Gauguins boarded a ship for the long journey back to France.

When he started boarding school in Orleans, a city south of Paris, Gauguin couldn't even speak French. He didn't like his new home or his school. Life in the gray, gloomy city of Orleans felt very different from that in Peru. In Lima, he had been free to do as he pleased. In Orleans, he had to submit to discipline. And the other students at his school were so ordinary, the children of common shopkeepers, he thought. These boys and girls didn't share the interesting experiences of his childhood. He wasn't a very good student, not because he wasn't smart, but because he was so arrogant. He was so sure that he was better than all the other students that he never even bothered to study. His high opinion of himself didn't win him many friends.

Sailing Away

Gauguin had one dream—he wanted to be a sailor. When he was 17 years old, he quit school and joined the merchant marines. Later, he joined the French Navy. For six years Gauguin sailed the oceans, visiting interesting ports all over the world.

PAUL GAUGUIN

Women Bathing

1885

At age 23 he decided to settle down. But what would he do for a job? The answer came from a friend of his mother's named Gustave Arosa. Arosa was a wealthy Parisian businessman and a talented photographer as well as a patron of the arts. He owned a large collection of paintings by some of the finest artists of the time. Arosa found Gauguin a job in Paris working for a stockbroker.

Even though Gauguin had no experience or training, he soon became very good at his job. It wasn't long before he was making a very good living for himself. He became a rich and respected broker. Life outside of his job was quiet. Gauguin's favorite pastime was reading. One day a friend from work, Émile Schuffenecker (Schuff, for short), got him interested in another hobby—painting.

A Sunday Painter

Gauguin immersed himself in his new hobby. Sometimes he and Schuff went on art outings together. Some days they went to the Louvre; other times they visited the galleries of art dealers. A few galleries had the courage to show the work of the "moderns"—the much-abused Monet and Renoir and their group. Often on Sundays they took their paint boxes and easels to the countryside outside Paris. Once in a while they even took an art lesson.

It was all great fun for Gauguin. With his puffed-up ego, he liked hearing others admire his work. One fall day in 1872, he found something else that made him happy. Her name was Mette Gad. Gad was on vacation in Paris when she first met Gauguin. Her home was Copenhagen, Denmark. Gauguin was immediately attracted to this tall, 22-year-old Danish girl. She had a lively personality and wasn't shy like many of the French girls he met. As for Gad, the more she learned about Gauguin, the more she liked him. He had such an interesting past, she thought. And now he was a wealthy stockbroker! The one thing Gauguin didn't mention to Gad was his interest in painting. Strangely, he waited to tell her until after they were married one year later.

At first, Mette didn't mind her husband's painting. She didn't realize that it was more than just a hobby, but, as time went on, it became all Gauguin thought about. Three years after their marriage, Gauguin entered one of his landscape paintings at the annual Salon. Not only was it accepted, the critics liked it! Meanwhile, Mette watched with growing concern the way in which Gauguin's hobby was turning into an all-consuming passion. She tried to remind him of his duties as a husband and a father—they now had a son. But her complaints had the opposite effect. He just spent more time painting. As for Gauguin, he tried to communicate his love for painting to his wife, but without success. Later, in his letters to Mette he often scolded her for her utter disinterest in anything

artistic and for her "silly concerns about money, pretty dresses, and neighborhood gossip."

One day, while visiting Arosa, Gauguin was introduced to another guest. It was the Impressionist artist Camille Pissarro. Like Arosa, Gauguin had started to collect art and had purchased paintings by Cézanne, Monet, Renoir, and Pissarro. When Pissarro heard that Gauguin was himself interested in painting, he invited Gauguin to paint with him. Soon, Pissarro became Gauguin's art teacher, and the first lesson he taught Gauguin was to use pure, bright colors.

Pissarro also took him to the Paris café where the modern painters and writers met to discuss their ideas. Not all the artists welcomed the newcomer. Monet didn't care for Gauguin and made little secret of it. He said he didn't approve of amateurs mixing with professionals. He and Renoir disliked the wealthy stockbroker's personality, too. Degas, on the other hand, enjoyed Gauguin's company, maybe because they were both a bit arrogant. Cézanne, who was always suspicious, absolutely hated Gauguin. "This fool of a Sunday painter is trying to filch hard-won secrets," he protested.

Nonetheless, Pissarro and Degas asked this Sunday painter to exhibit his work with the Impressionists. His debut was at the Fourth Impressionist Exhibition in 1879, where he submitted a sculpture. The next year he exhibited six

paintings. Although Gauguin had a high position on the stock exchange he was happiest when rubbing elbows with the professional artists, and he actively helped to sell their canvases. Over the next few years, he continued to paint, exhibited his work, sculpted, and took up ceramics, which he was very good at. "One day," he dreamed, "I'll become a full-time artist."

Life as an Artist

An unplanned event made Gauguin's decision to become a full-time artist much easier. In 1882 the Union General bank crashed and caused the stock market to collapse. It also caused Gauguin's income to decrease. Several months later he decided to quit. "From now on I paint every day," he declared when he got home. His wife was shocked. After all, he had a family to support—they now had five children. Besides, she was accustomed to living the life of a wealthy woman. As for Gauguin, he couldn't imagine failing at anything he tried. He was sure he would be an immediate success. But he was mistaken. Life as an artist was a tremendous struggle, and within a year their savings were used up. Angrily, Mette moved back to Denmark with their children. There she took a job teaching French.

Penniless, Gauguin became dependent on Schuff and a few others who occasionally offered

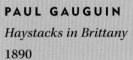

PAUL GAUGUIN

Haystacks in Brittany

1890

him hospitality and lent him money. Despite the setbacks and humiliations, Gauguin never wavered from his devotion to art. He never doubted that someday he would receive the recognition he deserved. He dreamed of traveling to a primitive place with a warm, sunny climate. There, he could live off the land and paint wonderful pictures. Eventually he was able to raise enough money to move to his tropical paradise—the island of Martinique. This Caribbean island, with its brilliant colors and friendly natives, delighted him. He lived in a cabin in a land he described as paradise. "Below us, the sea bordered by coconut trees, overhead every sort of fruit tree," he wrote to Mette in one of many letters. There was one serious problem, however. The damp, tropical climate proved devastating for Gauguin's health. He developed malaria, a debilitating disease that is transmitted by the bite of a mosquito. Gauguin suffered terrible attacks of chills and fevers, along with abdominal pain and diarrhea from an intestinal disease called dysentery. After four months, he had to return to France for medical treatment. But all had not been lost. During his time on the island, he completed 10 luminous paintings in a style that would soon be recognized unmistakably as his own.

Gauguin loved bright colors. He knew how bright colors could get from his days in sunny Martinique. He used these colors even if he wasn't

PAUL GAUGUIN
Detail from *Nave Nave Moe (Delightful Drowsiness)*
1894

painting a bright, sunny scene. "How do you see these trees?" he asked. "They are yellow? All right, put in yellow, the bluish shade, paint it pure ultramarine; those red leaves, use vermilion."

Gauguin also spent time painting on the coast of France, in a region called Brittany. He lived in a village called Pont-Aven. Artists from all over the world visited this area during the warm summer months. One summer, when Gauguin was 40, he met a young artist named Émile Bernard. Bernard was only 20, and he looked at Gauguin as his master. They became close friends, painting together and discussing art. Bernard liked to visit medieval churches to study their beautiful stained-glass windows. Soon the paintings of the two friends began to resemble stained-glass windows. They used brilliant flat colors, bounded by heavy black outlines. The colors looked more intense when they were outlined in black. Gauguin and Bernard were also influenced by other art forms such as folk art, tapestries, and Japanese prints. They experimented with perspective, using techniques they saw in these works.

Gauguin's art was different from the Impressionists' art in other ways, too. He thought a painting should do more than just show a scene. It should also express how the artist felt about the scene. "Don't copy nature too literally," he wrote in a letter to Schuff. "Draw art from nature as you

Activity

Cup of Gauguin

Gauguin was accomplished at many types of art. Pottery was one of his favorites.

Look at this detail from Gauguin's painting Delightful Drowsiness *and you'll see how he outlined his shapes in a dark color. He used this stained-glass style of painting to create designs on ceramic vases, too. This style of painting is called* cloisonnism. *Try out this technique using a foam cup as your vase.*

Materials
Styrofoam cup
Pen with black ink
Acrylic paints
Paintbrush
Container of water

1. Gently press into a foam cup with a black pen as you outline a design.
2. Add color to the outlined picture, allowing the black lines to show through. Use bright or perhaps even unnatural colors as Gauguin did for familiar objects. What effect does this outlining have on the objects in your drawing?

PAUL GAUGUIN
Detail from *Nave Nave Moe*
(Delightful Drowsiness)
1894

107

dream in nature's presence." Along with the colors he chose, Gauguin added symbols in his pictures to express his emotions. In his painting *Delightful Drowsiness*, for instance, he added a halo around the sleepy girl's head.

Other painters admired Gauguin's work so much that they began to paint in a similar style. They became known as the Pont-Aven School, and Gauguin was their leader.

A Visit to the South of France

Another artist who visited Brittany was named Vincent van Gogh. Van Gogh dreamed of starting a "Studio of the South" for artists. He invited Gauguin to live and share studio space with him in Arles, a village in southern France. Gauguin knew it was a bad idea. Their personalities were too different; they would never get along. On the other hand, van Gogh had a brother named Theo who was an important art dealer. "If I'm nice to Vincent," Gauguin thought, "Theo will try harder to sell my paintings." Against his better judgment, he made a deal. Gauguin agreed to move to Arles in return for Theo's support.

Vincent was thrilled. Life was lonely in his little yellow house. He set to work immediately decorating the house with paintings of yellow sunflowers to honor his guest.

PAUL GAUGUIN

Matamoe (Landscape with Peacocks)
1892

Even though van Gogh had an art dealer for a brother, only one of his paintings was sold during his lifetime, but today, van Gogh is one of the most beloved artists. His paintings sell for tens of millions of dollars. In fact, it was his painting *Portrait of Dr. Gachet* that received the highest price ever paid for a painting.

Both artists painted many pictures while they were in Arles. But it was a short visit for Gauguin. After two months of tension, van Gogh became so upset he tried to slash Gauguin with a razor. That night Gauguin thought it safer to sleep at a nearby hotel. When he returned home, neighbors surrounded the little yellow house—something was wrong with van Gogh. Gauguin found him curled up in bed under bloodstained sheets. Van Gogh had turned the razor on himself, cutting off part of his left ear. Because he bled so profusely, it was a miracle he was still alive. Gauguin summoned Theo and then left for Paris, badly shaken by the experience.

Off to Tahiti

In 1891, Gauguin returned to the tropics. This time he went to Tahiti. He would live in the islands, off and on, for the rest of his life. He always hoped

Activity

Armchair Explorer

Gauguin always dreamed of going to exotic places. In this painting game, you'll travel to an interesting place by using your imagination. Play by yourself or have a painting safari with your friends.

Materials

20 index cards
Pencil or pen
Paper
Drawing or painting supplies

1. Divide the index cards into four stacks of five cards each. On the first stack, write the word *Feelings* on each card. Repeat for the remaining three stacks of cards, writing the words *Character*, *Setting*, and *Condition*.

2. Turn the cards over. In the first stack, write a word that falls into the category of feelings. Write a different feeling on each card. Repeat for the remaining three stacks, but write different characters, settings, or conditions, depending on what pile you're marking. Here are some ideas:

   Feelings: happy, sad, lonely, peaceful, mysterious, scared, excited

   Character: wizard, dancer, athlete, bird, ghost, cat, space alien

   Setting: somewhere in the universe, castle, ocean, mountain, garden, zoo, island

   Condition: rainy, windy, sunny, starry night, full moon, misty, sunset

3. To play, shuffle each stack, then select one card from each stack. Close your eyes and imagine the scene that your cards describe. Paint a picture or make a sculpture that illustrates your set of words.

Another Impression: See how your imagination differs from those of the other artists playing the game. After you've made your piece of art, switch cards with the other players and create new pictures using their words.

he'd be wealthy again, and his family would join him in his tropical paradise. It was a dream that would never come true. Before leaving Paris he hired an art dealer, Ambroise Vollard, to sell his work. Occasionally, Gauguin sent Mette some money if he sold a painting, but this didn't happen very often.

Gauguin broke all the rules, in his art and in his life. In Tahiti, he found other girlfriends, even though he wasn't divorced from Mette. The first was a young native girl named Tehamana. Gauguin painted many portraits of her as well as vivid scenes from the island. After his first visit to France, he returned to find Tehamana married to someone else. He traveled to France occasionally, but he always returned to one of the islands in the South Pacific.

Back in Europe, most people failed to understand his art and, as a result, didn't like his paintings. During an exhibition, one woman screamed in horror when she saw a picture of a dog Gauguin had colored bright red. The reaction of the critics was a bit more encouraging. But some of them weren't ready for his use of unnatural colors. They made fun of his mustard-colored seas and vivid blue tree trunks.

Gauguin spent the last years of his life in poverty and pain. He broke his leg in a brawl during his last visit to France and became dependent on morphine and alcohol to escape from the excruciating pain. After suffering a series of heart attacks, Gauguin died at the age of 54. Gauguin was buried in a cemetery on Hiva-Oa, the last island he called home. It took three months for the word of Gauguin's death to reach Paris.

What happened to Mette? After her husband's death, she was finally able to sell many of his paintings. Once again she became a wealthy woman.

ART DETECTIVE

How to Spot a Gauguin
Here are some characteristics that will help you distinguish Gauguin's work:
- **Bright, flat colors!** Often outlined in black.
- **Unnatural colors!** They turn up in unexpected places.
- **Big white bonnets!** Women in Brittany wore this type of hat.
- **Writing on pictures!** Often, the picture's title is written somewhere on the painting.
- **Tropical scenes!** His favorite subjects include palm trees, native girls, and island motifs.

Gauguin's Legend Lives On

Five months after Gauguin's death, Vollard held an exhibition of his work. The public learned that Gauguin was far more than a colorful, exotic legend. Fifty paintings and 27 drawings revealed him to be an immensely powerful and strikingly original artist. Since that time, Gauguin's fame has grown even more. His bold use of color and form has influenced many of the artists who followed him, among them Pablo Picasso and Henri Matisse. Today, Gauguin is considered one of the most important contributors to modern art. He is remembered as an innovator, a courageous painter who dared to experiment.

PAUL GAUGUIN

Tahitian Landscape

1891

GEORGES SEURAT

Study for *Le Chahut*

1889

Georges Seurat

"I painted like that because I wanted to get through to something new—a kind of painting that was my own." This is how the timid young artist explained his paintings. But the new something wasn't at all what many of the older artists, including Monet and Renoir, wanted to be part of. When others in the group insisted on including the "something new" in the Eighth Impressionist Exhibition, it signaled the end of the group of revolutionary artists who had become known as the Impressionists. Although the organizers promised to set the "offending" art apart in its own room, Monet and Renoir refused to be associated with this quiet but determined artist.

On May 15, 1886, the Eighth (and last) Impressionist Exhibition opened its doors. The crowds came to applaud or scorn the paintings that offered a new impression. The young artist who caused all the fuss was Georges Seurat.

The End of an Era

The are many reasons why the Eighth Exhibition was the last for the Impressionists as a group. After the First Impressionist Exhibition caused such commotion, the artists had their ups and downs for several years. Now, 12 years later, many of them were finally being appreciated for their fresh, colorful paintings. Even the Salon had to accept that the Impressionists were here to stay. What's more, the Salon was losing its hold on the art market as smaller, private exhibits became popular. Also, art dealers who represented the Impressionists often held their own exhibitions.

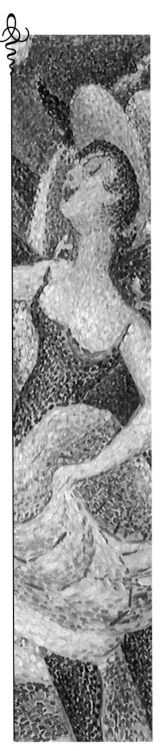

The artists were no longer the cohesive (although opinionated) group who had once met at the Café Guerbois. Back then, their main mission had been to escape from the Salon. Now, their disagreements were too strong to overcome. Some even questioned the Impressionist style. Pissarro and many of his colleagues began to think the Impressionists' way of painting was not disciplined enough. Others, like Monet and Renoir, were unwilling to be grouped with artists who worked in a structured, scientific method, as Seurat did.

A Quiet Young Artist

Seurat was much younger than the originators of Impressionism. He was just a boy when Monet and his group of radicals shook up the art world. At the time, young Seurat was a shy 14-year-old who enjoyed doodling on his sketch pad. Who would have guessed that, 12 years later, it would be his painting that caused all the stir?

Seurat was born in Paris on December 2, 1859. His mother came from a family of artisans. Some of her relatives were sculptors, and her father and grandfather were jewelers. She was a quiet, docile woman who ran the household and brought up the children.

Seurat's father, a legal official, was well off enough to retire when he was only 41. If you think

PAUL SIGNAC

Seurat met Paul Signac when they were both in their twenties. The two artists became close friends even though they had very different personalities. Seurat was quiet and reserved while his friend was very outgoing and exuberant. When it came to their art they were more similar. Signac admired Seurat's ideas and experimented with his painting technique, which is called *pointillism*. Pointillism is a painting technique of placing tiny dots of pure color next to one another so that at a distance, the viewer's eye mixes them. Signac's work was also included in the last Impressionist Exhibition. To the untrained eye of some critics, the work of the two artists looked the same.

Because Seurat was such a quiet man, he didn't say or write much about his life. But Signac wrote prolifically, and his letters, articles, and even his diary tell us many of the things we know about Seurat today.

that this gave him more time to spend with his family, you are mistaken. He was a secretive, solitary man who preferred to live in his own apartment, seven miles away from the Seurat household. He saw his wife and children every Tuesday evening when he came for dinner. Sometimes Georges would invite his friend, Paul Signac, to join them.

Dinner at the Seurats' was an exciting event. Seurat's father had lost his arm in a hunting accident, and he wore a mechanical device. "At mealtimes he screwed knives and forks into the end of this arm, which enabled him to carve legs of mutton, fillets (of beef), poultry, and game with speed, verve even," Signac remembered. "He positively juggled with these sharply pointed weapons, and when I was sitting next to him, I was terrified for my eyes." Meanwhile, Seurat paid no attention. He once drew his father at a meal, and the picture doesn't show these wild antics.

Despite the Tuesday evening meals, Seurat grew up in a quiet, middle-class household. His older brother and sister left home when he was a child, and sadly, his younger brother died at age five.

Seurat began drawing lessons when he was 16 years old. The classes were given at a school that taught decorative arts, such as ornamental sculpture. His teacher believed that drawing was the basis for all arts, and he taught Seurat how to draw from plaster casts and live models. Seurat also

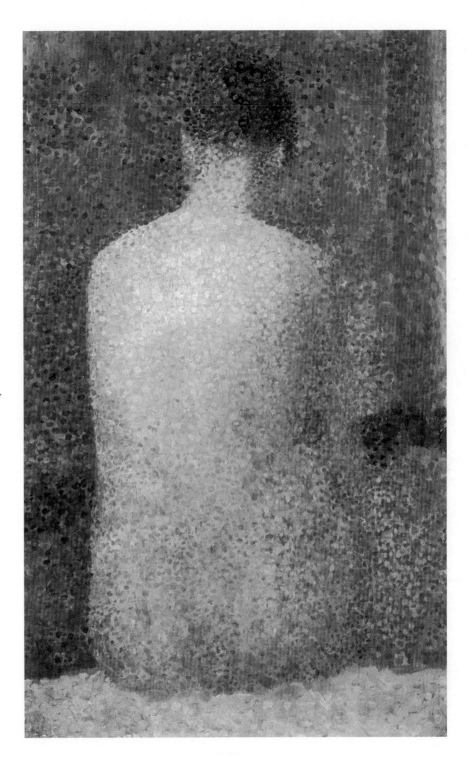

GEORGES SEURAT

Seated Model Seen from the Back
(study for *The Models*)
1886–87

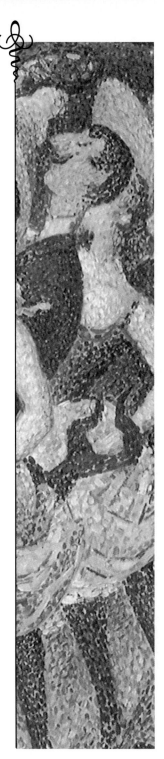

practiced by copying famous drawings. Two years later, he took an entrance exam for the École des Beaux-Arts. At age 18 he was admitted into this, one of the world's most prestigious art schools. It was a school that prided itself for teaching traditional art.

But Georges Seurat was not a traditional artist. At the end of the day, when his art lessons were over, Seurat would climb the great staircase of the École and enter the library. There, he'd go right on working, reading all he could about art and science. One of his favorite authors was Charles Blanc, who thought art and science should be combined. Blanc believed art could be achieved through a scientific method. Seurat started thinking about how he might do this.

Gradually Seurat realized that art school would not teach him what he needed to learn. When students at the École asked their teacher to let them sketch outdoors, the teacher said, "Oh! Yes, I know it's the thing to do nowadays, but first of all work as the Masters did, in studio lighting; when you've left the École you'll do as you please." After 18 months of study, that's just what Seurat did. He left the École, saying his lessons were "foolishly simple and incomplete." Another event convinced him it was time to leave. He had just seen an art exhibit that changed his life—the Fourth Impressionist Exhibition.

Seurat rented an art studio and began to "do as he pleased." Luckily, he wasn't under pressure to sell his artwork. His monthly allowance of 400 francs from his father was more than twice what the average industrial worker made. Seurat could take his time experimenting with a style he could call his own.

An Artist Who Loved Science

Seurat continued his scientific research and found that many discoveries about color were being made at that time. One of his favorite experiments was done by a physicist in Scotland named James Clerk Maxwell. Maxwell painted two colors on a disk, one on each side. He discovered that they blended together when the disk was spun very rapidly. A blue and yellow disk would look green when spun.

An American physicist, Ogden Rood, thought that you didn't have to spin a disk. From a distance, small dots of different colors blended together. This effect is called *optical mixing*.

These ideas had been explored earlier in tapestry weaving. A tapestry is a woven design made with colored strands of yarn. The finished piece is used as a wall-hanging. Eugène Chevreul, a chemist at a French tapestry factory in the early 1800s, worked with the dyes used to color the yarn.

GEORGES SEURAT

The Shore at Bas-Butin, Honfleur

1886

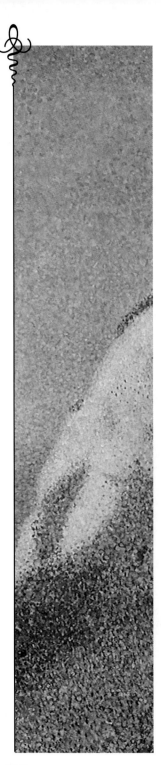

PIXELS AND POINTILLISM

The screen of a computer monitor or television screen contains many tiny dots called *pixels*. Although we see many colors on the screen, there are only three colors of dots: red, green, and blue. All the colors we see are made up of combinations of these three colors. A bunch of purple grapes, for instance, is an assortment of red and blue pixels. Because the pixels are so small, we see them as a solid image. A computer monitor or television screen is a bit like a Seurat painting.

He wondered why his colors sometimes looked faded. Then he realized that they hadn't faded at all. They just looked faded when put next to another color of yarn. He discovered that the strands' colors looked different depending on which color yarn was placed next to them. Like Rood, Chevreul observed that the eye blended adjoining colors. He also noticed that a color standing alone is surrounded by a faint halo of its complementary color. *Complementary colors* sit opposite each other on a color wheel. For instance, blue and orange are complementary colors. Chevreul noticed that blue strands had a faint halo of orange surrounding them. He wrote about his discoveries in 1839, 20 years before Seurat was born.

Seurat was also interested in a new field of science—the science of the mind. Today, it's called psychology. Around 1880, a man named Charles Henry started writing about the psychological effects of color and line. Seurat shared Henry's opinion that the elements in a picture had a psychological effect on its viewer. Henry had a theory that color and line could change our moods. For example, dark colors (also called cool colors) such as blue and purple make us feel sad. On the other hand, light colors (also called warm colors) such as yellow and red make us feel cheerful. The angle of a line makes a difference, too. Upturned lines are happy, while downward ones are gloomy.

From all these experiments, discoveries, and theories, Seurat developed a painting technique that was truly his own. It all came down to a simple dot.

Seurat's Methods

If ever there was an artist who had patience, it was Georges Seurat. Seurat decided to paint entire pictures using small dots. Instead of mixing colors on his palette like other artists, he let the viewer's eye mix his tiny dots. Painting with small dots, or points, is called *pointillism*.

Seurat's most famous painting took up an entire wall. This is the painting that was exhibited at the Eighth Impressionist Exhibition.

GEORGES SEURAT

*A Sunday on La Grande
Jatte—1884*

1884–1886

The picture Seurat made was of a beautiful park scene. He called it *A Sunday on La Grande Jatte.* And it was grand! This huge canvas was almost 7 feet tall and 10 feet wide (2.1 m by 3 m). Seurat needed a ladder to reach the top. He worked on this painting, dot by tiny dot, for two years until it was finished. When you see this picture in person, the colors seem to sparkle and dance.

It's not surprising that Monet didn't want to include Seurat with the Impressionists. Seurat's method of painting was very different from Monet's. Seurat was very methodical about what he put on his canvas. Each dab of his brush was carefully thought out, instead of the quick, spontaneous brush strokes of Monet. Unlike Monet, Seurat made many studies of a scene before he painted a final version. Seurat did spend time painting outdoors, but only to make preliminary sketches. After many months of study, he began his painting of *La Grande Jatte*—inside his studio.

Seurat made the studies for *La Grande Jatte* at the park. Each day he would set up his easel and concentrate on the scene in front of him. He was often too preoccupied to greet his friends when they passed by. But he didn't hesitate to ask them to cut the grass when it grew too long in the park.

Seurat even painted a frame of dotted colors around many of his pictures. He thought that traditional gold frames would detract from the colors in his pictures. To the painting of *La Grande Jatte* he added a three-centimeter (about 1½ inch) border of blue, red, and orange dots. The dots aren't evenly distributed, though. Where dark green touches the border, for instance, Seurat used more red dots in the border. And where orange touches the edge, there are more blue dots. He thought these complementary colors worked the best to show off his painting.

Many artists recognized that Seurat's ideas were important. Some, like Pissarro, tried to use his technique, but there was a problem: it took a very long time to paint a picture using tiny dots. Most artists didn't have the patience, and they went on to paint in other styles.

The Early Death of a Private Artist

Seurat didn't have much to say unless it was about his art. "His was an extremely withdrawn personality," wrote his artist friend Charles Angrand. When

> "If I had to describe him in one word, I would say that he was above all an organizer, in the artistic sense of the word. Hazard, luck, chance, the sensation of being carried away—these things meant nothing to him."
> —Belgian poet Émile Verhaeren, speaking of his friend Georges Seurat

friends came to visit his studio, Seurat ignored them and continued to paint. He would perch on his stepladder in front of a huge canvas, eyes half closed, working in silence. Tired of being ignored, Seurat's friends sometimes started arguing about his theories. This got his attention! He'd step down from his ladder, pick up a piece of chalk, and begin to draw on the studio floor. He'd draw lines—sad, happy, and indifferent—and color wheels—every complementary in its proper place. In a slow, even voice, Seurat would talk about his method, pointing out the things he believed absolutely.

When it came to his private life, however, Seurat never confided in his friends. Even his closest friends didn't know he had a girlfriend named Madeleine Knobloch, and that they had a baby son. Seurat's friends only learned about his small family after his unexpected death.

Seurat was only 31 years old when he became ill with fever and suddenly died. It's now thought that he was stricken with meningitis, an inflammation of the brain and spinal cord. His 13-month-old son died from the same illness a few days later.

Art Detective

How to Spot a Seurat

Here are some characteristics that will help you distinguish Seurat's work:

- **Dots!** Look closely at the painting and you'll see thousands of tiny dots.
- **Frame of dots!** Many paintings are surrounded by a border of dots that frame the picture.
- **Huge!** Seurat's most famous paintings are very large.
- **Practice makes perfect!** Once you get to know Seurat's finished pieces, you'll recognize the many mini pictures he made preparing for them. You'll find these preliminary experiments hanging in museums, too.

Seurat's Task Was Completed

Seurat didn't leave many paintings behind because each one took so long to complete. Today, many people would agree with what his good friend Paul Signac wrote in his diary: "Some critics say that Seurat didn't leave a life's work behind him, but it seems to me that, on the contrary, he gave what he had to give, and gave it admirably. He would certainly have painted many more pictures, and made further headway, but his task was completed." Seurat's vibrant dots of color continue to dazzle us today.

Seurat Sugar Cookies

Here's a piece of art that you can eat. Decorate these delicious cookies using Seurat's painting technique. Make each cookie into a sugar-sprinkled masterpiece.

Makes about 36 cookies
Adult help suggested

Ingredients

1 cup butter or margarine
  (2 sticks)

1 cup sugar

2 tablespoons milk

1 teaspoon vanilla extract

2 1/2 cups all-purpose flour

Utensils

Large mixing bowl

Electric mixer

Clear plastic wrap

Rolling pin

Cookie cutters

Cookie sheets

Decorating Materials

Food coloring

Water

Small bowl for each color

Cotton swabs

Sugar

1. In a large mixing bowl, beat the butter or margarine until it becomes softened. Add the sugar and beat until fluffy. Add the milk and vanilla. Beat well. Gradually beat in the flour.

2. Divide the dough into four parts and wrap each part in clear plastic wrap. Chill in the refrigerator for at least 1 hour.

3. Preheat the oven to 375° F. On a lightly floured surface, roll out one piece of dough until it's 1/4-inch thick. Use floured cookie cutters to cut out shapes. Place them on ungreased cookie sheets. Repeat with the remaining dough.

4. Mix a small amount of food coloring with a few drops of water. Repeat using a separate container for each color. Dip a cotton swab into one color and dab it onto the cookies, making small dots. Add dots of other colors, experimenting with combinations, as Seurat would. Sprinkle with sugar.

5. Bake at 375° F for about 8 minutes or until the edges are light brown. Remove the sheets from the oven and let them cool for 1 minute. Place the cookies on a cooling rack.

Another Impression: In place of food coloring, decorate with other types of cake decorations such as jimmies, colored sugar crystals, or chopped gum drop pieces. Sprinkle several colors onto the cookies in a pointillist style.

GUSTAVE CAILLEBOTTE

Sculls on the Yerres

1877

Lasting Impressions

It's been a hundred years since Monet and his group shocked the world with their paintings. It's hard to believe that these bright, colorful pictures once caused such a negative stir. Luckily, the young artists kept painting despite the critics' disdain. Their canvases fetch millions of dollars today and are among the most recognized artworks in the world.

Each artist contributed his or her unique style to the Impressionist Movement.

Monet's emphasis was on landscapes. He concentrated on how light played and reflected off his subjects, rather than the subjects' details.

Renoir specialized in portraits of beautiful women, happy children, and people enjoying life. "Paintings should be likable, joyous, and pretty," he said, and he used luscious colors and shapes to prove his point.

Degas worked behind the scenes, showing less familiar aspects of Parisian life. We see young, aspiring ballerinas hard at work. Degas's paintings emphasize their effort rather than the glamour of public performance.

Cassatt was limited in her choice of subjects because she couldn't venture out the way a man could. We see images of home life, such as mothers and children enjoying quiet times together. The portraits are unposed and relaxed, as if seen through a window.

The artists who became known as the Post-Impressionists took what they learned from the Impressionists and went a step further.

GUSTAVE CAILLEBOTTE

The artist who painted *Sculls on the Yerres* isn't as famous as Claude Monet, but he played an important role in the lives of the Impressionists. Gustave Caillebotte was a wealthy man, and he helped support Monet and many other artists. He gave them money when they needed it and bought their artwork. When he died he willed his collection to the Louvre. It included masterpieces by all the Impressionists but, unbelievable to us today, it was turned down. Eventually the Louvre was persuaded to accept about half the collection; the rest of the masterpieces are in other lucky museum collections throughout the world.

Cézanne wanted to make something solid out of Impressionism. He painted bright canvases, using patches of color and simple geometric shapes. It was a few steps before Cubism, which is why he is called the father of Modern Art.

Gauguin chose a new subject, the brightly lit scenes and people of the tropics. His canvases feature intense, flat colors with subjects outlined in black.

Seurat created an entirely new technique of painting, utilizing new theories of color. His can-

vases were covered with thousands of tiny dots of color, which make the picture sparkle.

Today, many Impressionist paintings are considered masterpieces. They are shown in museums all over the world, waiting for you to visit them.

Here are some ideas to make your museum visits more fun. Carry your art games in the Art-to-Go Knapsack that is described on page 19. Don't forget the game described on page 76 titled "Every Picture Tells a Story." Add a small sketch pad and some drawing materials to your knapsack. With these you'll be ready to draw a copy of your favorite painting on your next museum visit, just as the Impressionists did at the Louvre.

Impressionism Blooms

Today, an exhibition of Impressionist paintings will draw people from all over the world. If Claude Monet could give you a tour of one of these exhibits, he'd tell stories about the struggles his group faced to get these paintings where they are today. After your tour, he might take you to see the art that followed Impressionism. Here you'd discover how the next generation of artists was influenced by Monet's group. Younger artists experimented with the colors and shapes of the Impressionists, but they created their own new

CLAUDE MONET

Houses at Argenteuil

1873

TEMPLE OF THE MUSES

The word *museum* comes from the word *muse*. According to Greek mythology, Zeus had nine daughters who were called the muses. They were the goddesses of creativity. The Greek word *mouseion* means a "temple to the muses."

styles. The bright colors of the Impressionists were the starting point for Henri Matisse and others who created a style called *Fauvism* that used bright colors and less realistic forms and shapes in their artwork. Cézanne's patches of color inspired Pablo Picasso to develop Cubism. Monet's experiments with how the sun lit up objects paved the way for *abstract art*, which features only color and shape, but not the objects at all.

After your tour through the museum, Monet might invite you to a local café. There, you could discuss and debate your ideas about art, just as in the old days at the Café Guerbois.

CLAUDE MONET
Detail of *Houses at Argenteuil*
1873

You don't have to go to a museum to see Impressionist paintings. To learn more about Monet and his group, visit these Web sites.

Monet and the Impressionists for Kids On-Line

http://members.aol.com/sabbeth/monet.html

Additional on-line resources from the author of *Monet and the Impressionists for Kids*. Hear Impressionist music, print out patterns for projects, and link to other great sites.

The Art Institute of Chicago Collections

www.artic.edu/aic/collections/index.html

Take a tour of the museum's collection of Impressionist paintings. To locate the French Impressionists and Mary Cassatt, click on both the European and American collections.

Café Guerbois

www.cafeguerbois.com

Meet the Impressionists at their favorite hangout, the Café Guerbois. Click to see what and where the artists painted. Learn about the artists who came before them and provided inspiration.

Edgar Degas at the Metropolitan Museum of Art

http://metmuseum.org/explore/degas/html/index.html

Explore the life, times, and work of Edgar Degas. View his own art collection of works by other artists.

Explore Monet's World

www.mfa.org/monetsworld/

Take a journey to London, Venice, and Giverny. Learn why these places were so special to Monet and explore the paintings he created there. Play interactive games and send e-postcards, Monet style.

The First Impressionist Exhibition, 1874

www.artchive.com/74nadar.htm

Enter the exhibition and click on an artist's name. You'll explore some of the paintings shown at the First Impressionist Exhibition and read what the critics had to say.

Giverny—Claude Monet's House and Gardens

www.giverny.org/gardens

An on-line visit to Claude Monet's home. See photos of his house and explore his beautiful gardens.

Mary Cassatt at the Metropolitan Museum of Art

http://metmuseum.org/explore/cassatt/html/index.html

Explore the life, times, and work of Mary Cassatt.

Museum of Fine Arts, Boston

www.boston.com/mfa/monet

An on-line tour of the museum's special exhibition of Monet in the 20th century.

National Gallery of Art, Washington D.C.

www.nga.gov/collection/gallery/french19.htm

Take a tour of works by Monet, Renoir, Gauguin, Cassatt, and other French painters of the 19th century. Audio is available on some of these tours.

Welcome to Claude Monet's

www.intermonet.com

Learn about the life and art of Monet in either English or French.

Picture Me

Stand in front of a painting that has one or more people in it. You might wonder, as you scan the picture, what it would be like to be in it. Where would you be standing? Perhaps you would be sitting or lying down. What would you be wearing? Is it hot or cold out? Sunny or stormy? In the game, each player should choose his own painting and make up a story. When everyone is finished, listen to each story as you look at its picture.

Bingo Monet

This game is like regular Bingo, but you must find your answers in Impressionist paintings.

Materials

Large index cards	Scissors
Fine tip color markers	Clear plastic tape
Pencil	Pencil eraser
String	

1. Using a fine-tip marker, draw a grid on an index card with four boxes across and four boxes down. In three boxes, write the word *Complementary*. In the remaining boxes, write the following words:

   Warm, Cool, Landscape, Portrait, Self-Portrait, Still Life, Pointillism, Plein Air, Bird's Eye View, Pastel, Cropped Image, Seascape, FREE.

2. Decorate each box with colors or images that describe the word it contains.

3. Cut a string about 12 inches (30 cm) long. Tape one end to a pencil and the other end to the index card.

4. Make one card for each player.

5. To play the game, go to the Impressionist section of the museum. Take your index card. As you explore the paintings, keep in mind the words on your card. When you see something in a painting that is listed on your card, then make an *X* in that box. The first person to find four items in a row must take everyone on a tour to see the answers. Erase the check marks from each box to play again.

Another Impression: For an easy version of this game, fill each box with the name of a color or combination of colors to search for. See if you can find all of the colors in the same painting.

Picture Plugged In

Stand in front of a painting at the museum. A picture of a group of people or a landscape works best. Take a moment to scan the picture. Notice the details, such as the time of day, setting, and any emotion the artist may be trying to express. If there are people in the picture, note what they are doing and where each individual is looking. Pretend the picture is a scene from a movie, and if you push a button, the action will begin. Take turns telling the story of what happens in the picture. Everyone playing the game can add to the story until the movie comes to an end.

Art Critic

At the museum, give each member in your group two blank index cards and a pencil. On one side, write your name. On the other side, write "least favorite" on one card and "most favorite" on the other. Look at all the Impressionist paintings. Each player should secretly choose his or her most favorite and least favorite painting. Next, everyone places the proper card, name side up, on the floor in front of the paintings they chose. As you revisit those paintings together, each person should explain his or her choice. There are no wrong answers in this game. All of you have your own ideas about what you like and don't like.

Glossary

Abstract art: a style of art that is based on the idea that elements of a picture, such as color, shape, and form, have visual value on their own, without representing a recognizable subject.

Advance: to come closer. In a painting, a color can make an object seem closer to the viewer. Things that are colored red, yellow, or orange seem to advance.

Background: the part of a picture that appears to be farthest away from the viewer.

Bird's-eye view: looking down on a scene from above.

Bourgeois (boor-JWA): a French word meaning "middle class." It also implies an unimaginative attitude, overly concerned with luxuries.

Candid shot: a photograph of someone who is not posing.

Caricature: a drawing of a person that exaggerates his or her features for comic effect.

Cloisonnism: a style of painting, created by Paul Gauguin and others, where shapes are outlined in dark colors to create a two-dimensional flat pattern.

Collage: a picture made of pasted and overlapping pieces of paper.

Color wheel: a circular arrangement of the primary colors (red, yellow, and blue) and their mixtures.

Complementary colors: a pair of colors that sit opposite each other on the color wheel. When next to each other, each color makes the other seem more intense. Red and green, yellow and purple, and blue and orange are pairs of complementary colors.

Composition: the way an artist arranges elements in a picture.

Cool colors: those colors where blue is dominant, including greens and purples.

Cropping: cutting off the edge of a picture.

Cubism: an art movement started around 1907 by Pablo Picasso and Georges Braque that breaks a picture down into geometric shapes. Images are depicted at many different angles at once.

Cuisine: the French word for "kitchen." Today, the word is used to describe a certain style of preparing food, such as French cuisine.

Decoupage (day-koo-PAHZH): a French term that means "cutting out." This art form originated in France in the 17th century as a way to decorate bookcases, cabinets, and other pieces of furniture. It became a fashionable pastime in 18th-century French courts.

Fauvism: a style of art that began around 1905 and used brilliant colors to express emotion. Portraits, landscapes, and other motifs were painted in bright, unnatural colors. Henri Matisse was the leader of this movement, which lasted only a few years. The word *fauve* means "wild beast" in French.

Flaneur (flah-NOOHR): a French term that describes a well-dressed gentleman out for a stroll.

Foreground: the part of a picture that appears to be closest to the viewer.

Framing: in photography, aiming the camera so that the picture includes just what the photographer wants.

Galette (gah-LEHT): a thin, round French cake. There are many types of galettes. *Galette des Rois* is a traditional cake served during Twelfth Night festivities and contains a bean or other token guaranteed to bring the recipient good luck.

Highlight: a bright spot in a picture.

Horizon line: the line where sky and earth appear to meet.

Hue: the actual color of something, identified by a common name such as red or greenish yellow.

Landscape: a picture of natural scenery.

École des Beaux-Arts: French for "the School of Fine Arts."

Louvre (LOO-vruh): located in Paris, it's one of the largest and most famous art museums in the world. It was originally built as a residence for the king of France. Today it exhibits some of the world's greatest art treasures.

Middle distance: the part of a picture between the foreground and background.

Museum: comes from the word *muse*. According to Greek mythology, Zeus had nine daughters who were called the muses. They were the goddesses of creativity. The Greek word *mouseion* means "a temple to the muses."

Palette: a thin oval board, with a thumb hole and finger grip at one end, on which a painter arranges his or her colors.

Pastels: chalk-like colored crayons made of powdered pigment bound with gum. The pictures made with these crayons are also called pastels or pastel paintings.

Perspective: the method used by artists to make a flat surface look as if it has depth.

Pixel: the screen of a computer or television monitor contains many tiny dots, called pixels. There are three colors of dots: red, green, and blue. All the colors seen on a monitor are made up of these three colors. Because the pixels are so small, together they appear as a solid image.

Plein air: a French term that means "open air" or "outdoors."

Pointillism: the technique of placing tiny dots of pure color next to one another so that, from a distance, the viewer's eye mixes them together.

Porcelain: a ceramic material that is famous for its translucent qualities. It's made from a special type of clay that is mixed with a paste. Vases, cups, and plates made of porcelain are considered very fine quality.

Portrait: a picture or sculpture of a particular person.

Recede: to move away from. In a painting, a color can make an object seem farther away. Things that are colored blue, green, and purple seem to recede. This is true in nature, too. Moisture in the atmosphere makes distant objects seem bluer or grayer.

Reflection: the reproduction of an image by, or as if by, a mirror. In many of Monet's paintings, clouds and trees appear as reflections in the water.

Rococo: an art movement that was popular in the 1700s in the court of King Louis XV. It's known in general for excessive decoration, ornament, and curlicues. Paintings were of fun, light-hearted scenes with themes such as love and courtship.

Seascape: a picture featuring the sea.

Self-portrait: a picture or sculpture that an artist makes of him- or herself.

Shadow: a dark shape cast by an object blocking the light. The Impressionists often painted shadows in the complementary color of the object. A woman wearing a yellow dress would cast a purple shadow.

Snapshot: a quick, casually taken photograph.

Still life: a picture of a group of inanimate objects, arranged by the artist. It's usually set indoors and contains a man-made object, such as a tabletop or vase.

Viewpoint: the position from where a scene is viewed.

Voilà (vwa-LA): a French exclamation that means "see there." It's used to express approval, or to suggest an appearance as if by magic.

Warm colors: those colors where red and yellow are dominant, including orange.

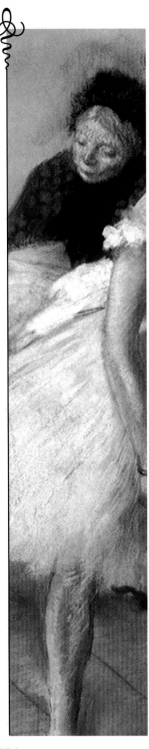

Bibliography

Bade, Patrick. *Degas*. London: Studio Editions Ltd., 1992.

Cain, Michael. *Mary Cassatt*. New York: Chelsea House Publishers, 1989.

Denvir, Bernard. *The Chronicle of Impressionism*. London: Thames and Hudson Ltd., 1993.

Greenfield, Howard. *First Impressions: Paul Gauguin*. New York: Harry N. Abrams, Inc., Publishers, 1993.

Hanson, Lawrence and Elisabeth. *Noble Savage: The Life of Paul Gauguin*. New York: Random House, 1954.

Howard, Michael. *Gauguin*. New York: Dorling Kindersley, Inc., 1992.

Knapp, Ruthie, and Janice Lehmberg. *Museum Guides for Kids*. Worcester, MA: Davis Publications, Inc., 1998.

Mancoff, Debra. *Mary Cassatt: Reflections of Women's Lives*. New York: Stewart, Tabori & Chang, 1998.

Mount, Charles Merrill. *Monet*. New York: Simon and Schuster, 1966.

Muhlberger, Richard. *What Makes a Cassatt a Cassatt?* New York: The Metropolitan Museum of Art, Viking, 1994.

Muhlberger, Richard. *What Makes a Monet a Monet?* New York: The Metropolitan Museum of Art, Viking, 1993.

Patin, Sylvie. Monet: *The Ultimate Impressionist*. London: Thames and Hudson Ltd., 1993.

Prather, Marla, and Charles F. Stuckey. *Gauguin: A Retrospective*. New York: Park Lane, 1989.

Renoir, Jean. *Renoir, My Father*. Boston: Little, Brown and Company, 1962.

Rewald, John. *Cézanne*. New York: Harry N. Abrams, Inc., 1986.

Rewald, John. *The History of Impressionism*. New York: The Museum of Modern Art, 1973.

Rewald, John. *Seurat*. New York: Harry N. Abrams, Inc., 1990.

Russell, John. *Seurat*. London: Thames and Hudson, Ltd., 1965.

Salvi, Francesco. *The Impressionists*. New York: Peter Bedrick Books, 1994.

Shapiro, Barbara Stern. *Pleasures of Paris: Daumier to Picasso*. Boston: Museum of Fine Arts, Boston, 1991.

Spence, David. *Cézanne: The Analytical Brush*. Tunbridge Wells, Kent, Great Britain: Ticktock Publishing Ltd., 1998.

Spence, David. *Degas: The Invisible Eye*. Tunbridge Wells, Kent, Great Britain: Ticktock Publishing Ltd., 1998.

Spence, David. *Manet: A New Realism*. Tunbridge Wells, Kent, Great Britain: Ticktock Publishing Ltd., 1997.

Spence, David. *Renoir: Colour & Nature*. Tunbridge Wells, Kent, Great Britain: Ticktock Publishing Ltd., 1998.

Thompson, Brenda, and Michael Howard. *Impressionism*. New York: Smithmark Publishers, Inc., 1992.

Thomson, Richard. *Seurat*. London: Phaidon Press, 1985.

Venezia, Mike. *Pierre Auguste Renoir*. Chicago: Children's Press, 1996.

Venezia, Mike. *Monet*. Chicago: Children's Press, 1996.

Image Credits

All images courtesy of Wood River Gallery except for * courtesy of The Art Institute of Chicago. The collection and location names are included for reference.

Page x
Claude Monet
The White Water Lilies
1899
oil on canvas
The Pushkin Museum,
Moscow

Page 2
Pierre Auguste Renoir
The Ball at the Moulin de la Galette
1876
oil on canvas
Musée d'Orsay, Paris

Page 5
Claude Monet
Impression, Sunrise
1872–73
oil on canvas
Musée Marmottan, Paris

Page 9
Claude Monet
Boulevard des Capucines
1873–74
oil on canvas
The Nelson–Atkins Museum
of Art, Kansas City, Missouri

Page 10
Edgar Degas
Dancers Preparing for an Audition
c. 1880
pastel on paper
The Denver Art Museum,
Colorado

Page 11
Berthe Morisot
The Cradle
1872
oil on canvas
Musée d'Orsay, Paris

Page 13
Gustave Caillebotte
Paris: A Rainy Day
1877
oil on canvas
The Art Institute of Chicago

Page 16
Édouard Manet
Bar at the Folies-Bergère
1881–82
oil on canvas
Courtauld Institute
Galleries, London

Page 18
Édouard Manet
On the Beach at Boulogne
1868
oil on canvas
Virginia Museum of Fine
Arts, Richmond

Page 22
Claude Monet
Cliff-walk at Pourville
1882
oil on canvas
The Art Institute of Chicago

Page 25
Claude Monet
The Stroll, Camille Monet and Her Son Jean (Woman with a Parasol)
1875
oil on canvas
National Gallery of Art,
Washington, D.C.

Page 28
Claude Monet
Regattas at Argenteuil
1872
oil on canvas
Musée d'Orsay, Paris

Page 32
Claude Monet
*London, The Houses of
Parliament: Stormy Sky*
1904
oil on canvas
Musée des Beaux Arts, Lille

Page 34
Claude Monet
*The Artist's Garden at
Vetheuil*
1881
oil on canvas
National Gallery of Art,
Washington, D.C.

Page 36
Claude Monet
The Luncheon
c. 1874
oil on canvas
Musée d'Orsay, Paris

Page 37
Claude Monet
Pool of Water Lilies
1900
oil on canvas
The Art Institute of Chicago

Page 39
Claude Monet
Haystack in Winter
1890–91
oil on canvas
Museum of Fine Arts,
Boston

Page 42
Claude Monet
Water Lilies
1906
oil on canvas
The Art Institute of Chicago

Page 44
Pierre Auguste Renoir
The Umbrellas
1881–85
oil on canvas
National Gallery, London

Page 52
Pierre Auguste Renoir
*Portraits of Children
(The children of Martial
Caillebotte)*
1895
oil on canvas
Private Collection

Page 54
Pierre Auguste Renoir
Dance in the City
1883
oil on canvas
Musée d'Orsay, Paris

Page 55
Pierre Auguste Renoir
*The Artist's Son Jean
Drawing*
1901
oil on canvas
Virginia Museum of Fine
Arts, Richmond

Page 58
Edgar Degas
*Café-Concert at the
Ambassadeurs*
c. 1876–77
pastel over monotype
Musée des Beaux Arts,
Lyons

Page 62
Edgar Degas
Blue Dancers
1897
pastel on paper
The Pushkin Museum,
Moscow

Page 67
Edgar Degas
Dancers at the Bar
c. 1876–77
oil on canvas
The Metropolitan Museum
of Art, New York

Page 70
Mary Cassatt
The Bath
1891–92
oil on canvas
The Art Institute of Chicago

Page 73
Mary Cassatt
*Lydia Leaning on Her Arms,
Seated in a Loge*
c. 1879
pastel on paper
Private Collection

Page 76
Mary Cassatt
Young Mother Sewing
c. 1900
oil on canvas
Metropolitan Museum of
Art, New York

Page 78
Mary Cassatt
The Letter
1890–91
drypoint and aquatint on
paper
National Gallery of Art,
Washington, D.C.

Page 81
Mary Cassatt
The Cup of Tea
1879
oil on canvas
The Metropolitan Museum
of Art, New York

Page 83
Paul Gauguin
*Matamoe (Landscape with
Peacocks)*
1892
oil on canvas
The Pushkin Museum,
Moscow

Page 84
Paul Cézanne
*Still Life with Curtain and
Flowered Pitcher*
c. 1898–99
oil on canvas
The Hermitage Museum,
St. Petersburg

Page 90
Paul Cézanne
Still Life with Three Peaches
1885–87
oil on canvas
American ambassador's
residence, Paris. On loan
from the National Gallery of
Art, Washington, D. C.

Page 91
Paul Cézanne
View of Gardanne
1885–86
oil on canvas
The Brooklyn Museum,
New York

Page 95
Paul Cézanne
Houses in Provence
(*Vicinity of L'Estaque*)
1879–82
oil on canvas
National Gallery of Art,
Washington, D.C.

Page 98
Paul Gauguin
Nave Nave Moe (*Delightful
Drowsiness*)
1894
oil on canvas
The Hermitage Museum,
St. Petersburg

Page 102
Paul Gauguin
Women Bathing
1885
oil on canvas
National Museum of
Western Art, Tokyo

Page 105
Paul Gauguin
Haystacks in Brittany
1890
oil on canvas
National Gallery of Art,
Washington, D.C.

Page 108
Paul Gauguin
Matamoe (*Landscape with
Peacocks*)
1892
oil on canvas
The Pushkin Museum,
Moscow

Page 111
Paul Gauguin
Tahitian Landscape
1891
oil on canvas
Minneapolis Institute of Arts

Page 112
Georges Seurat
Study for *Le Chahut*
1889
oil on canvas
Albright-Knox Art Gallery,
Buffalo, New York

Page 115
Georges Seurat
*Seated Model Seen from the
Back* (study for *The Models*)
1886–87
oil on wood
Musée d'Orsay, Paris

Page 117
Georges Seurat
*The Shore at Bas-Butin,
Honfleur*
1886
oil on canvas
Musée des Beaux-Arts,
Tournai

Page 119
Georges Seurat
French
1859–1891
A Sunday on La Grande Jatte
1884*
1884–86
oil on canvas
207.6 x 308 cm. Helen Birch
Bartlett Memorial Collection.
1926.224. Photograph courtesy of The Art Institute of
Chicago

Page 120
Georges Seurat
The Circus
1890–91
oil on canvas
Musée d'Orsay, Paris

Page 124
Gustave Caillebotte
Sculls on the Yerres
1877
oil on canvas
National Gallery of Art,
Washington, D. C.

Page 127
Claude Monet
Houses at Argenteuil
1873
oil on canvas
National Gallery, Berlin

Index

A

abstract art, 128
Académie Suisse, 27
arts, patronage of the, 6

B

Barbizon School, 16
Bartholdi, Frédéric Auguste, 17
Bazille, Frédéric, 28, 31
Bernard, Émile, 107
Blanc, Charles, 116
Boudin, Eugène, xi, 24–25

C

Café Guerbois, 29, 61, 88, 114, 128
Caillebotte, Gustave, 13, 124, 126
   Paris: A Rainy Day, 13
   Scull on the Yerres, 124, 126
caricature, 24
Cassatt, Mary, xii, 11, 37, 64–65, 70–81,
   85, 125
   The Bath, 70
   Cézanne, Paul, and, 85
   characteristics of paintings by, 80
   childhood of, 71–72, 74
   The Cradle, 75
   The Cup of Tea, 81
   Degas, Edgar, and, 64–65, 74–75, 80
   École des Beaux-Arts and, 74
   etchings by, 78
   the Fourth Impressionist Exhibition
     and, 75
   influence of Japanese art upon,
     78–79
   the Legion of Honor Medal and, 80

   The Letter, 77–78
   life in Beaufresne, 80
   life in Paris, 74–75
   *Lydia Leaning on Her Arms, Seated
     in a Loge*, 73
   methods of painting, 75–78, 125
   and the Pennsylvania Academy of
     Fine Arts, 72
   Portrait of Madame Cortier, 71
   the Salon and, 74–75
   Women's Pavilion of the World's
     Columbian Exhibition mural, 79
   the Women's Suffrage Movement
     and, 79
   Young Mother Sewing, 76
Cézanne, Paul, xii, 38, 82, 84–97, 128
   bartering of art for food and, 91
   Cassatt, Mary, and, 85
   characteristics of paintings by, 96
   childhood of, 86–87
   Fiquet, Hortense, and, 92–93
   the First Impressionist Exhibition
     and, 94
   the Fourth Impressionist Exhibition
     and, 104
   Gaugin, Paul, and, 104
   House of the Hanged Man, 11
   *Houses in Provence (Vicinity of
     L'Estaque)*, 95, 97
   life in Paris, 87–88
   life in Provence, 92
   methods of painting, 88–92, 97, 126
   Pissarro, Camille, and, 88
   *Still Life with Curtain and Flowered
     Pitcher*, 84, 86
   Still Life with Three Peaches, 90

   the Third Impressionist Exhibition,
     and, 94
   View of Gardanne, 91
   Vollard, Ambrose, and, 93
   Zola, Émile, and, 86–89
Charigot, Aline. *See* Renoir, Pierre
   Auguste
Charpentier, Marguerite, 49, 56
Chevreul, Eugène, 116, 118
cloísonnism, 107
complementary colors, 40, 118
cool colors, 90, 118
Corot, Camille, 16
Cubism, 96, 128

D

Debussy, Claude, 14
Degas, Edgar, xii, 8, 10, 14, 31, 58–69, 71,
   74–75, 77, 80, 125
   Absinthe, 15
   Blue Dancers, 62–63
   Café-Concert at the Ambassadeurs,
     15, 58
   Cassatt, Mary, and, 64–65, 74–75, 80
   characteristics of a painting by, 69
   childhood of, 59–60
   Dancers at the Bar, 66–67
   Dancers Preparing for an Audition,
     10, 69
   the First Impressionist Exhibition
     and, 64–65
   Gaugin, Paul, and, 104
   life in Italy, 60
   life in Paris, 61
   Little Dancer of Fourteen Years, 65

Manet, Édouard, and, 61
methods of painting, 10, 62–63, 65,
   68, 125
Monet, Claude, and, 62
paintings of ballerinas, and, 65
Rehearsal of a Ballet on Stage, 10
sculpture and, 65
the Sixth Impressionist Exhibition
   and, 65
*The Sufferings of the City of New
   Orleans*, 61
de Laboulaye, Édouard, 17
Doncieux, Camille. *See* Monet, Claude
Durand-Ruel, Paul, 33

E

Eastman, George, 68
École des Beaux-Arts, 6, 27, 77, 116
Elder, Louise. *See* Havemeyer, Louise
en plein air (in the open air), 16, 92
etching, process of, 78

F

Fauvism, 96, 126
Fiquet, Hortense. *See* Cézanne, Paul
Franco-Prussian War, 4, 33

G

Gad, Mette. *See* Gaugin, Paul
Galette des Rois, 57
Gaugin, Paul, xii, 82, 98–111
   Cézanne, Paul, and, 104
   characteristics of paintings by, 110
   childhood of, 101–103

Degas, Edgar, and, 104
Fifth Impressionist Exhibition and, 99, 104
Fourth Impressionist Exhibition and, 104
Gad, Mette, and, 103–104, 110
Haystacks in Brittany, 105
life as a merchant marine, 101
life as an artist, 104–110
life as a stockbroker, 103
life in Arles, 108–109
life in Martinique, 106
life in South America, 100–101
life in Tahiti, 109–11
Matamoe (*Landscape with Peacocks*), 83, 108
methods of painting, 107–108, 126
Monet, Claude, and, 99, 104
Nave Nave Moe (*Delightful Drowsiness*), 106–107
Pissarro, Camille, and, 104
Renoir, Pierre Auguste, and, 99, 104
the Salon, and, 103
painting as a hobby, 103
Pont-Aven School, and, 108
Tahitian Landscape, 111
van Gogh, Vincent, and, 108–109
Women Bathing, 102
Gleyre, Charles, 15, 27–28, 47

H

Haussmann, Baron, 12, 15
Havemeyer, Louise, 80–81
Henry, Charles, 118
Hoschedé, Alice, 35–36
Hoschedé, Ernest, 35
Hugo, Victor, 101

I

Impressionist composers, 14
Impressionist Exhibitions, xii, 17–18, 65, 82
  Eighth, 113, 118
  Fifth, 99
  First, 4, 8, 34, 48–49, 64–65, 71, 75, 94, 113
  Fourth, 37, 75, 104, 116
  Seventh, 36
  Sixth, 65
  Third, 94

J

Japanese art, 64, 77

K

Knobloch, Madeleine. *See* Seurat, Georges
Kodak camera, 68

L

"A Limited Company of Painters, Sculptors, and Engravers," 8–9
Louis-Napoléon, Bonaparte. *See* Napoléon III, Emperor

M

Macchiaioli, 60
Manet, Édouard, xii, 34, 61, 88
  Bar at the Folies-Bergère, 14, 16
  Degas, Edgar, and, 61
  Le Déjeuner sur l'Herbe (*Luncheon on the Grass*), 7, 35
  Morisot, Berthe, and, 75
  Olympia, 61
  On the Beach at Boulogne, 18
Matisse, Henri, 96, 111, 128
Maxwell, James Clark, 116
Monet, Claude, xi–xii, 8–9, 16, 22–43, 45, 62, 64, 75, 85, 88, 92, 113–14, 126, 128
  The Artist's Garden at Vetheuil, 34–35
  Boudin, Eugène, and, 24–25
  Boulevard des Capucines, 9, 19
  the Café Guerbois and, 29, 31
  characteristics of a painting by, 41
  childhood of, 23–25
  Cliff-walk at Pourville, 22
  Degas, Edgar, and, 62
  Doncieux, Camille, and, 31, 33, 35–36
  the Fifth Impressionist Exhibition and, 99
  the Fourth Impressionist Exhibition and, 37
  Gaugin, Paul, and, 99, 104
  Haystack in Winter, 39–40
  haystacks, painting of, 38
  Houses at Argenteuil, 127–28
  Impression, Sunrise, 4–5, 9, 21, 34
  life in Argenteuil, 33
  life in Giverny, 36–39, 41
  life in London, 33
  life in Paris, 27–28
  London, The Houses of Parliament: Stormy Sky, 32
  The Luncheon, 36
  methods of painting, xi, 21, 26, 29–30, 40, 89, 125
  Pool of Water Lilies, 37
  Regattas at Argenteuil, 28, 30
  Renoir, Pierre Auguste, and, 47–48
  the Salon and, 31, 99–100
  Seurat, Georges, and, 120, 129
  the Seventh Impressionist Exhibition and, 36
  The Stroll, Camille Monet and her Son Jean (*Woman with a Parasol*), 25–26
  Water Lilies, 42
  The White Water Lilies, x
Morisot, Berthe, 10–11, 75
  The Cradle, 11
  Manet, Edgar, and, 75
Musée de l'Orangerie, 41
museum, meaning of, 128

N

Napoléon III, Emperor, 12, 17, 61, 100–101

O

Ondine, 14
on the line, definition of, 7
opera-ballet, 12
optical mixing, 116

P

Palmer, Bertha, 79
Paris, renovation of, xii, 12, 14–15, 61
Paris Autumn Salon, 96
perspective, 90–92
Picasso, Pablo, 96, 111, 128
Pissarro, Camille, 88, 93, 104, 114, 121
pixels, 118
pointillism, 114, 118
Post-Impressionists, xii, 81–124

R

Ravel, Maurice, 14
Renoir, Pierre Auguste, xii, 9–10, 14, 16, 28, 31, 38, 44–57, 61, 64, 75, 85, 88, 92, 113–14
  The Artist's Son Jean Drawing, 55
  The Ball at the Moulin de la Galette (*Au Moulin de la Galette*), 2–4, 20, 51, 63
  characteristics of paintings by, 56
  Charigot, Aline, and, 53–54, 56
  childhood of, 45–46
  Dance in the City, 54
  family life and, 51, 53
  the Fifth Impressionist Exhibition and, 99
  the First Impressionist Exhibition and, 48–49
  Gaugin, Paul, and, 99, 104
  La Logue, 9–10
  life as a porcelain painter, 46
  life in Cagnes, 54, 56
  methods of painting, 48–49, 51, 89, 125
  Monet, Claude, and, 47–48
  Portraits of Children, 50, 52
  The Umbrellas, 44, 49, 56
Rood, Ogden, 116
Rouart, Henri, 66

S

Salon, the, 6–7, 31, 33–34, 61, 71, 74–75, 93–94, 99–100, 103, 113–14
Salons des Refusés (Salon of the Rejected), 7
Seurat, Georges, xii, 82, 112–22
  characteristics of a painting by, 122
  childhood of, 114–16
  The Circus, 120
  Eighth Impressionist Exhibition and, 118
  Fourth Impressionist Exhibition and, 116
  Knobloch, Madeleine, and, 121
  methods of painting, 118, 120–21, 126
  Monet, Claude, and, 120, 129
  Seated Model Seen from the Back, 115
  The Shore at Bas-Butin, Honfleur, 117
  study for *La Chahut*, 112
  A Sunday on La Grande Jatte, 119–21
Signac, Paul, 114
Sisley, Alfred, 28, 85
skyed, definition of, 7
Statue of Liberty, 17, 28

T

Tanguy, Julien, 91
Tournachon, Félix (Nadar), 8–9

U

Ukiyo-e. *See* woodblock prints

V

van Gogh, Vincent, xii, 4, 108–109
  Portrait of Dr. Gachet, 4, 109
van Gogh, Theo, 108–109
Vollard, Ambroise, 93, 110–11

W

warm colors, 90, 118
woodblock prints, 64, 77

Z

Zola, Émile, 86–89